Scenic Driving

VIRGINIA

Bruce Sloane

FALCON®

HELENA, MONTANA

A **FALCON** GUIDE ®

Falcon® is continually expanding its list of recreational guidebooks. All books include detailed descriptions, accurate maps, and all the information necessary for enjoyable trips. You can order extra copies of this book and get information and prices for other Falcon guidebooks by writing Falcon, P.O. Box 1718, Helena, MT 59624 or calling toll-free 1-800-582-2665. Please ask for a free copy of our current catalog. Visit our website at www.FalconOutdoors.com or contact us by e-mail at falcon@falcon.com.

© 1999 Falcon® Publishing, Inc., Helena, Montana.
Printed in the United States of America.

1 2 3 4 5 6 7 8 9 0 MG 04 03 02 01 00 99

Falcon and FalconGuide are registered trademarks of Falcon® Publishing, Inc.

Front and back cover photos by Jeff Greenberg.
Front cover: Mount Rogers National Recreation Area
Back cover: Virginia Beach

Library of Congress Cataloging-in-Publication Data
Sloane, Bruce, 1935–
    Scenic Driving Virginia / Bruce Sloane
        p.   cm.
    Includes index.
    ISBN 1-56044-731-1 (pbk.)
       1. Virginia—Tours. 2. Automobile travel—Virginia—Guidebooks
I. Title.
F224.3.S58 1999   98-55773
917.5504'43—dc21   CIP

CAUTION

All participants in the recreational activities suggested by this book must assume responsibility for their own actions and safety. The information contained in this guidebook cannot replace sound judgment and good decision-making skills, which help reduce risk exposure; nor does the scope of this book allow for disclosure of all the potential hazards and risks involved in such activities.

Learn as much as possible about the recreational activities in which you participate, prepare for the unexpected, and be cautious. The reward will be a safer and more enjoyable experience.

 Text pages printed on recycled paper.

Contents

Acknowledgments

Profound thanks go to my wife, Joy, my personal chauffeur and companion as we crisscrossed the state. She is the one who made sure I always had the needed maps, film, camera, tape recorder, and paper and pencils when we embarked. She is also the draftsperson—she took what started as my scratches on a road map and turned them into reasonable drafts of maps for Falcon's cartographers to finalize.

I am indebted to Blue Ridge Parkway Ranger E. L. Sutton at Cumberland Knob, North Carolina, who gave me several hints about Virginia. Several rangers at Fredericksburg Battlefield helped me devise a more or less scenic route through the battlefields that avoided suburbia as much as possible.

Joy and I are also grateful to another anonymous ranger near Roanoke for his encyclopedic gustatory knowledge of the French, Italian, Chinese, Indian, and American restaurants of Roanoke.

Locator Map

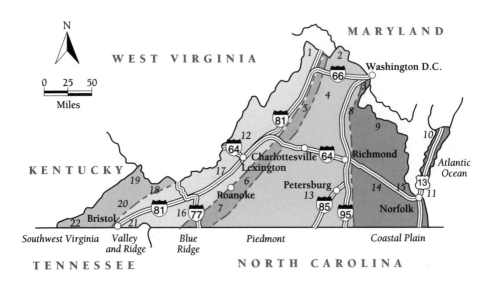

Map Legend

Scenic Drive - paved		Interstate	
Scenic Drive - gravel		U. S. Highway	
Scenic Side Trip - paved		State and County Roads	
Scenic Side Trip - gravel		Forest Service Roads	000
Interstate		Pass	
Other Roads (paved)		Butte, Mesa, or Spire	
Other Roads (gravel)		Peak and Elevation	9,782 ft.
Railroad		Glaciers	
Airport		Wilderness Area National/State Park	
Junction			
Bridge		National Forest Boundary	
Building			
Point of Interest		State Boundary	W A
Campground		Map Orientation	
Cliff			
Hiking Trail		Scale of Miles	0.5 Miles
River/Creek		Boat Launch	
Waterfall		Picnic Area	
Lake			

Since 1926, more than 1,500 historical markers have been placed throughout the state to add to travelers' knowledge and interest.

Introduction

. . . it's that time when the pull of the blue highway is strongest, when the open road is a beckoning, a strangeness, a place where a man can lose himself.

William Least Heat Moon
Blue Highways

I remember the many automobile trips I took with my parents when I was a young boy. I would stand up in the back seat behind my father, the driver (this was in the days before seat belts, when back seats had enough room for small boys to stand, and four-lane highways were rare), and chat with him as we rode along.

We would talk about many things, but mostly we discussed the scenery—the hills, houses, barns, fields, mountains, lakes, rivers, and small towns we slowly passed through. Time seemed suspended, and all that existed in my young universe was the car, the scenery, and my father's company. I never wanted the trip to end, whether it was a few hours or several days; for me (and I think for him) the voyage was more important than the destination.

Today a trip by car is more often a frustrating, bumper-to-bumper commute or a high-speed cruise down a concrete strip as wide as a football field. Cars are faster and better built. Modern roads and modern cars have taken much of the romance and adventure out of driving, much as crowded and cramped airliners and airport hassles have muted the miracle of flight.

But unspoiled roads still exist, and Virginia has its share. Twenty-two of them are described in this book. From Chincoteague in the northeast corner to Cumberland Gap in southwest Virginia, scenic roads abound. Some, like Skyline Drive and the Blue Ridge Parkway, are world famous. Others are little-known byways that take you through the hidden corners of the state.

Along these roads you'll encounter mountains and valleys, thick forests, caves, sandy beaches, abundant bird life, small towns, fishing villages, and picturesque farms. Virginia's roads also reflect the state's rich and proud history. You'll see the first permanent white settlement in the New World, colonial mansions, Civil War battlefields, and the birthplaces of several presidents.

Virginia, the Old Dominion state, is rightfully proud of its road system. Even though the state ranks 35th in size among the 50 states, it has the country's fifth-longest highway system. Most drives are along paved and well-maintained two-lane or four-lane roads and can be safely traversed by motor homes or cars pulling camper-trailers. The few mountain roads and dirt roads that are not suitable for these types of vehicles are clearly noted in the text; most of these are side trips that can be omitted from the main drive. Except for Skyline Drive, the Blue Ridge Parkway, and some national forest and battlefield roads, all roads are numbered.

Extending almost the full length of the state is the 2,000-mile-long, Georgia-to-Maine footpath, the Appalachian Trail (AT). About 150 people hike the entire AT each year, and millions more hike along some portion of it. More than 600 miles of the AT—about one-third of the total mileage—lie within Virginia. Several drives cross or parallel the AT, giving you numerous opportunities for short or long hikes.

Hiking is a popular activity in the Old Dominion state, and except for the highest mountain areas, it can be indulged in almost year-round. Hikes along many drives are described here. For a description of 52 hikes throughout the state, including many not mentioned here, see the FalconGuide *Hiking Virginia* by Randy Johnson.

Virginia extends 200 miles north to south and about 500 miles east to west. Its varied topography and geography range from coastal estuaries and beaches in the east to mountains more than 5,000 feet high in the south and west. Scenic drives cover all portions of the state and were selected to display the most interesting scenic, historical, and unique features. Many drives extend into two or more sections. From east to west, geologists divide the state into the sections shown below; the drives that pass through each section are given.

Tidewater and Coastal Plain. Virginia's Coastal Plain includes the land areas adjacent to the Atlantic coastline, both shores of Chesapeake Bay, and the tidal reaches of the Potomac, James, Rappahannock, and other rivers. An area of low relief, it is underlain by unconsolidated, sandy sediments and encompasses the bays, estuaries, offshore islands, and saltwater marshes along the coast.

Virginia's Coastal Plain was the site of the first European settlements in North America, and it played a vital role in the birth and early years of the United States. Today it includes the thriving cities of Williamsburg, Newport News, Norfolk, and Virginia Beach, and surrounding areas, including the beaches and bird-watching areas of the Eastern Shore and the Northern Neck. Drives 3, 8, 9, 10, 11, 14, and 15 lead to scenic, historic, and natural points of interest on Virginia's Coastal Plain.

Piedmont. The tidewater ends at the Fall Line where the sediments of the Coastal Plain overlap the older crystalline rocks of the Piedmont. Because the rocks of the Piedmont are much harder than the soft, unconsolidated sediments of the Coastal Plain, they do not erode as easily, so rapids have formed in rivers as they cross this boundary. The Fall Zone marks the head of navigation on the rivers, where many of the major cities, such as Washington, D.C., Fredericksburg, and Richmond, were built. The Fall Zone is less prominent south of Petersburg.

The Piedmont stretches westward from the Fall Zone to the foothills of the Blue Ridge, covering a broad area of the state. The rocks here are deeply eroded with thick soil and rich farmlands. The northern Piedmont has rolling hills, flattening out in the southern part of the state. The blood of both Federal and Confederate troops drained into the soil of the Piedmont during numerous battles of the Civil War. Drives 2, 3, 4, 8, and 13 pass through at least part of the Piedmont.

Blue Ridge. The Blue Ridge is Virginia's easternmost range of mountains, including several peaks exceeding 4,000 feet in elevation. The Blue Ridge extends in an almost unbroken line the length of the state in a northeast-southwest line from the Potomac River in northern Loudoun County to the North Carolina-Tennessee border. The rocks of the Blue Ridge are mainly Precambrian metamorphosed sediments and lava flows.

Some of the most outstanding scenery and scenic drives in Virginia lie along the Blue Ridge and its ridgeline, including Skyline Drive and the Blue Ridge Parkway, drives 5, 6, and 7.

Valley and Ridge. The Valley and Ridge section consists of broad valleys and long, even ridgelines west of the Blue Ridge. It is made up of folded, faulted, and eroded Paleozoic sedimentary rocks. The ridges are underlain by sandstone, which is resistant to erosion; less resistant limestone and shale make up the valleys. The folding has in places resulted in five or six parallel ridgelines and adjacent valleys.

Immediately to the west of the Blue Ridge in the northern part of the state is the wide Shenandoah Valley, and its continuation farther south, the Great Valley. These limestone valleys are known for their numerous caves, many of which have guided tours. In the northern half of the state the Valley and Ridge extends into West Virginia; farther south it is bordered on the west by the Appalachian Plateau. The George Washington and Jefferson National Forests cover much of the area, particularly the heavily wooded ridges.

For convenience, Mount Rogers is placed here in the Valley and Ridge section, but its enigmatic, Precambrian geology puzzles earth scientists; some think it belongs in a province of its own. Scenic drives in the Valley and Ridge are drives 1, 12, 16, 17, 18, and 21.

Southwest Virginia. What is often referred to as Southwest Virginia is mostly part of the Appalachian Plateau, a region of high cliffs and thick, horizontal beds of sandstone with numerous seams of coal. The boundary between the Valley and Ridge and Southwest Virginia is vague and hard to distinguish in places.

The difference is that when the rocks of the Valley and Ridge were folded, the rocks of the Appalachian Plateau formed thrust faults; the rocks remained relatively flat, but slid over on top of each other like a spread-out deck of cards. Drives 18, 19, 20, and 22 pass through Southwest Virginia.

Virginia's climate east of the Blue Ridge is moderate and variable. In non-mountainous areas you can expect warm to hot summers and mild winters. The hottest region of the state is the southern Piedmont. In the Tidewater and Eastern Shore areas the climate is moderated by Chesapeake Bay and the Atlantic Ocean. Most parts of the state, particularly in the northern half, get a few snowstorms each winter; but, except for a blizzard every few years, the snow usually vanishes in a day or two.

The climate in the mountains of the western and southwestern areas of the state depends on the altitude. Summer temperatures in the high mountains are usually several degrees lower than in nearby lowlands. At higher elevations winter can be severe with heavy snows, and mountain roads can be closed for several days because of winter weather. The most severe weather is in the high country around Mount Rogers, where an average of more than 70 inches of snow falls each winter.

In addition, the weather—both summer and winter—can change quickly with changes in elevation, from summer-like conditions in the valleys to wintry conditions a few thousand feet higher. Summer thunderstorms are common. Because many of the mountain drives rapidly go up and down, you should be prepared for cooler weather at higher elevations.

With its varied habitats, Virginia also has diverse bird, animal, and plant life. Some 400 species of birds are known in the state. Migrating shore and wading birds follow the marshes and estuaries of the Eastern Shore; hawks, falcons, and passerine birds ride the thermals along the windswept ridges of the Blue Ridge on their semiannual journey. Bald eagles, one of the largest populations in the East, inhabit the estuaries of the Potomac, Rappahannock, and other rivers, and are also found in some mountain areas. The woods, forests, hills, and fields support a large and varied bird population.

The state also supports a rich mammal population. Two species of deer—the common Virginia whitetail deer, and Chincoteague's sika elk— plus raccoon, possum, skunk, a growing black bear population, and many smaller animals are found here.

The forests have thick growths of hardwoods and softwoods. Wildflowers bloom from early spring to late fall. Spring is especially beautiful when the majority of the wildflowers bloom, and the slopes are covered with blossoms of rhododendron, redbud, and mountain laurel.

The Virginia Department of Conservation and Recreation manages about 35 state parks and related sites throughout the state. Many parks are along or close to the drives and many are mentioned as points of interest. Some parks are free; others charge a modest day-use fee in season. Additional fees are levied for camping and lodging or for special use, such as the chair lift at Natural Tunnel State Park. For information on fees or to make reservations, call toll-free 800-933-PARK.

The George Washington and Jefferson National Forest (now operated under a single administration) covers 2 million acres of public land in western Virginia. Many drives pass through or around the forest. The Forest Service maintains numerous recreation areas and campsites, of which only a few are mentioned here. For detailed maps or other information, call the Forest Supervisor at 540-265-5100.

The National Park Service administers numerous sites in Virginia, both historic and scenic, including such diverse areas as George Washington's Birthplace National Monument and Shenandoah National Park. Phone numbers for additional information on these sites are given in the Appendix.

Virginia is steeped in history, from Jamestown to the Civil War. The Civil War permeates the state. Twenty-six major battles and more than 400 smaller engagements were fought on Virginia soil. Two drives cover specific campaigns and battles of that war, and many other drives mention Civil War sites along their routes.

The drives are described from a starting point to an end point, or from a starting point in a loop back to the starting point. However, you can begin most drives at many places along the route, or tour them from finish to start if that is more convenient.

Information for each drive starts with "General description," which gives a one-paragraph summary of the drive. "Special attractions" points to key features of the drive. "Location" ties the drive to a nearby large town or general area within the state, and "Drive route numbers" tell you the highway numbers covered by the drive. "Travel season" tells you the time of year when the drive looks especially attractive, such as during spring blossoming or autumn leaf changing. "Camping" points you to any private and public campgrounds along or near the drive. "Services" tell you where to get gas for the car and food and lodging for the motorists. For all but a few drives, these services are readily available at several places on the drive. Many points of interest are located off the drive; "Nearby attractions" will help you decide if you want to visit them.

Getting to scenic drives is made easy by Virginia's excellent interstate highways. I-81 and I-95 roughly cover the state from north to south, while I-64, I-66, and I-77 provide access east to west. And some portions of the interstates themselves are scenic: Mountainous I-77 is part of Drive 15.

The Appendix lists phone numbers and addresses of visitor information centers and some local points of interest. It is arranged numerically by drive for convenience.

. . . where has nature spread so rich a mantle under the eye? Mountains, forests, rocks, rivers. With what majesty do we there ride above the storms!

Thomas Jefferson
Notes on the State of Virginia

The Mabry Mill along the Blue Ridge Parkway has been grinding cornmeal and buckwheat since E.B. Mabry set up shop in 1910.

1

Shenandoah Valley Loop

Winchester-Luray-Strasburg-New Market

General description: This 110-mile loop tours much of the northern Shenandoah Valley from the valley floor to the ridgeline of the surrounding mountains. This tour provides you with varied, sweeping views alternately looking up at the mountains and down at the valleys. The route goes past small towns, both branches of the Shenandoah River, Civil War battle sites, and several caves with guided tours.

Special attractions: The star of the trip is the Shenandoah Valley itself and the surrounding Blue Ridge Mountains. Features include a trip along the ridgeline of Massanutten Mountain, the opportunity to visit some of the Shenandoah Valley's world-famous caves, a drive through a covered bridge, and several Civil War battlefields.

Location: The trip begins and ends at Winchester in the northwest corner of the state off Exit 313 of Interstate 81, about 10 miles from the West Virginia line.

Drive route numbers: U.S. Highways 522, 340, 211, and 11; Virginia Highways 600, 55, 678, 675, and 720.

Travel season: The trip can be made at any time of the year. Heavy snows in winter may temporarily close some mountain roads. Some facilities may be closed in winter.

Camping: Camping and trailer facilities are available at the Elizabeth Furnace Recreation Area in the George Washington and Jefferson National Forest, at several areas in Shenandoah National Park, and at Jellystone Park in Luray.

Services: Gasoline, motels, hotels, and restaurants are available in all towns along the route.

Nearby attractions: Shenandoah National Park and Skyline Drive (see Drive 5), various caverns, and Shenandoah Valley Music Festival.

 The Drive

The Shenandoah Valley of Virginia stretches for about 200 miles in a northeast-southwest line from the West Virginia panhandle to Roanoke. The valley was first settled by Europeans in the early 1700s who adopted the Indian name "Shenandoah," which means "daughter of the stars." It soon became a major farming area and corridor for westward expansion.

Drive 1: Shenandoah Valley Loop
Winchester-Luray-Strasburg-New Market

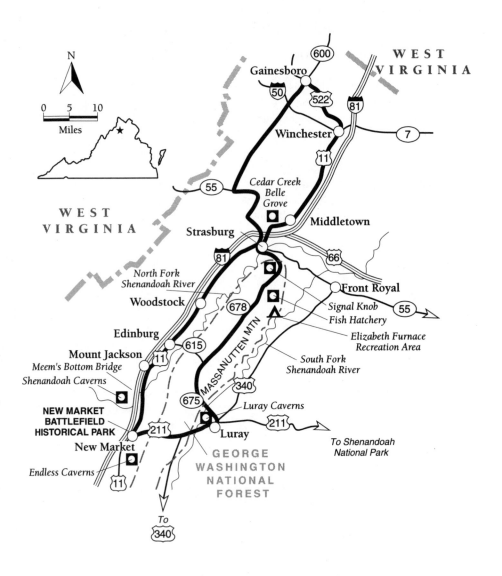

The valley lies between the Blue Ridge Mountains to the east and the Alleghenies to the west. Its rich, limestone soils continue to support Virginia's extensive apple orchards, fields of corn, soybeans, and other crops, and poultry farms. Much of the northern Shenandoah Valley is dominated by the long ridge of Massanutten Mountain, which divides the valley in two. The South Fork of the Shenandoah River drains the southeastern section; the North Fork of the Shenandoah River drains the northwestern. The two forks unite to become the Shenandoah River at Front Royal, which flows to Harpers Ferry, West Virginia, to join the Potomac River.

Below the valley floor several thousand caves have formed in the limestone and dolomite carbonate rocks; some of the biggest and most interesting provide guided, lighted tours for the public.

Because the valley was such an important farming area and was used as a thoroughfare for both Union and Confederate troops during the Civil War, several major battles and numerous smaller skirmishes and encounters took place here. Today the valley is traversed by high-speed Interstate 81, used by several million vehicles each year, and is paralleled by its aging predecessor, US 11.

The drive begins in the historic town of Winchester and follows back roads to Strasburg, "the Antique Capital of the Blue Ridge." You then cross the North Fork of the Shenandoah River and enter the George Washington National Forest. After traversing a short canyon you cross the twin ridges of Massanutten Mountain. As you descend the mountain, you have superb views of the South Fork of the Shenandoah and the fertile Shenandoah Valley.

The drive then joins US 211, passes by Luray Caverns, and crosses Massanutten Mountain again to New Market. You then head north on old US 11 with magnificent views of the Blue Ridge, past some of the bloodiest battlefields of the Civil War, and return to Winchester where the drive ends. Total mileage is about 110 miles. The trip can be made in one day, but if you stop to visit a cave, a battlefield, or historic site, you may want to take several days.

The town of Winchester has been rich in history since colonial days. The oldest building in town, known as Abram's Delight, has been restored to its original 1754 splendor and is open to the public, including an herb garden and formal boxwood garden. You can also visit George Washington's Office Museum, used by the young officer as both a surveying office and later as headquarters during the French and Indian wars.

More than 100 years later, the town, strategically located at the head of the Shenandoah Valley, was a pivotal spot during the Civil War. The valley provided a transportation corridor north and south, and its rich farmlands of food crops and—farther south—tobacco, were coveted by both sides. Winchester's importance is shown by the fact that the town changed hands some 72 times during the four-year conflict, reducing the town to shambles by the end of the war.

The Kurtz Cultural Center in Old Town Winchester is a good source of information about Civil War sites in the valley. The Center also honors two local home-grown heroes: Patsy Cline, the country music star who met an early and tragic end, and polar explorer Robert E. Byrd. Additional Civil War memorabilia is exhibited at Stonewall Jackson's headquarters, used by the Confederate general in 1861 in Winchester.

To begin the actual drive, head north from Winchester on US 522. Once out of town, this four-lane highway with its gentle curves and grades winds through several road cuts where the folded limestones, dolomites, shales, and mudstones that make up the valley floor are exposed.

At Gainesboro, about 10 miles from Winchester, the drive turns left onto two-lane VA 600. VA 600 winds through Gainesboro and heads into the open country. This narrow road passes farms of corn and hay and numerous herds of both dairy and beef cattle.

The level valley floor ends in hardwood ridges that parallel both sides of the road; most farms are maintained as open fields up to the steeper part of the ridge. These ridges, like most of the higher points in the Shenandoah Valley, are made up of sandstone rocks folded into an anticline, or arch. Because the sandstone does not erode as easily as the limestones, shales, and mudstones that underlie most of the valley, the sandstone forms resistant ridges.

Four miles from Gainesboro, VA 600 crosses four-lane US 50. Continue on VA 600 past the stop sign and several other stop signs farther along. Virginia 600 ends at VA 55 in about 13 miles. Turn left on VA 55, a broad two-lane road. The ridgeline you see ahead on the horizon stretching to the right is Massanutten Mountain. The prominent high point at the left hand end is Signal Knob, a Civil War observation and message station.

Cross I-81 and enter the town of Strasburg. The town calls itself "the Antique Capital of the Blue Ridge," with almost 100 antique dealers in the Strasburg Emporium on VA 55. Although they are busiest in the warmer months, most are open year-round. On Main Street is the Strasburg Museum and the elegant Hotel Strasburg, furnished to restore its 1890 Victorian splendor.

Follow VA 55 through town. For a few blocks the road parallels US 11 where you will return at the end of the driving loop. Virginia 55 soon leaves town and crosses the North Fork of the Shenandoah River. You are now at the base of Signal Knob whose steep slopes have been visible for many miles. The road curves gently around the mountain's wooded base.

At the other side of the mountain, about 5 miles past Strasburg, turn right on VA 678. Virginia 55 continues straight ahead to Front Royal, starting point for Skyline Drive (Drive 5). Continue on VA 678, which enters George Washington National Forest.

The forest name may confuse you. Originally there were two national forests in Virginia: George Washington National Forest, primarily in the northwestern part of the state and neighboring West Virginia, and Jefferson

National Forest in southwest Virginia and nearby parts of West Virginia. They have since been consolidated into one mouthful of an entity: George Washington and Jefferson National Forest. However, the northern section is still known as the George Washington section, and the southern section continues to be known as . . . right, you get the idea. Most maps and most people still refer to the original names.

At any rate, you enter thick woods in the national forest, and the road begins to climb. A road to the left leads to a fish hatchery. Many open views through the hardwood trees show conical peaks and cliffs to the left. Virginia 678 follows the small wooded canyon of Passage Creek with several unmarked parking areas and turnoffs for swimming, fishing, and picnicking. The creek bed flows over steeply dipping beds of sandstone, forming small rapids in places.

About 3.5 miles from VA 55, you pass the parking area and trailhead on the right for a 10-mile circuit hike to Signal Knob. Just past the trailhead, a road leads left to the Elizabeth Furnace Recreation Area, a hiking, camping, and picnic area; a trail here leads to the ridgeline of Massanutten Mountain.

After several miles the road leaves the creek bed and the grade steepens. You level off and emerge from the woods in a small valley with ridgelines to the left and right. This is the eroded axis, or center, of the anticline; the sandstone has been worn away here, like a truncated McDonald's archway. Most of the land here is privately owned although surrounded by the national forest. Lush farms alternate with woods.

About 10 miles from VA 55, go left on VA 675. The road narrows and climbs steeply with many bends up a wooded ridge. At the crest of the ridge, park at the side of the road and cross the road for an outstanding view of the fields and farmlands of the Shenandoah Valley east of Massanutten Mountain. The view includes the South Fork of the Shenandoah River, the town of Luray, and on clear days, the distant peaks of the Blue Ridge and Shenandoah National Park.

Past the viewpoint, VA 675 quickly descends to the valley floor. Turn left at the stop sign at the T-intersection at the edge of the South Fork of the Shenandoah River. You will see a bridge that crosses the river. Turn right over the bridge, still following VA 675.

Follow VA 675 into Luray, crossing over US 211. Unfortunately there is no access to US 211 here. Follow VA 675 through the outskirts of Luray to the stop sign at U.S. Highway 340. Turn left (north) on US 340. (Turn right to visit the town of Luray.) You will see US 211 a quarter of a mile ahead. Turn left on US 211 (west, toward New Market). (In the other direction, to the east, US 211 twists and climbs the Blue Ridge to Shenandoah National Park and Skyline Drive, intersecting Drive 5 in the middle; it then descends to the Piedmont at Sperryville in the middle of Drive 4.)

US 211 is a four-lane divided highway that will seem like a speedway after the narrow mountain roads. You are in a wide valley. The taller Blue

Massanutten Mountain looms above the fertile farmlands in the Shenandoah Valley.

Ridge Mountains are behind you to the east; Massanutten Mountain is straight ahead. On clear days mountains will stretch to the horizon in all directions.

In 2 miles you pass the entrance to Luray Caverns, the most famous, most popular, and most advertised cave in Virginia. Discovered in 1878, the cave was soon open to the public. It became immensely popular, attracting visitors from around the world, and the tourist money they brought was a major factor that helped the area recover from the ravages of the Civil War. The cave features large rooms and an underground organ, the "Stalacpipe," which strikes stalactites (which hang down from the ceiling) and stalagmites (which grow up from the floor) to generate musical tones. In addition to cave tours, the cavern properties include an old-time auto museum and bell carillon.

The carbonate rocks (limestone and dolomite) in which Luray Caverns and other caves are formed were deposited from organic material at the bottom of shallow tropical seas, during early Paleozoic time, some 300 to 500 million years ago. These seas were similar to the Bahama Bank that surrounds today's Bahama Islands.

The limestone and dolomite contain small amounts of the sulfide mineral pyrite. The caves were dissolved out by slowly percolating groundwater which contained small amounts of sulfuric acid from oxidation of the pyrite. The solution followed cracks and fissures in the rock, dissolving the limestone and dolomite, forming many caves with large rooms and spacious passages. The same groundwater also deposited calcite on the walls, ceilings, and floors of the caves, leaving festoons of stalactites, stalagmites, flowstone, and other picturesque formations.

All caves mentioned on this drive offer safe, comfortable, well-lighted guided tours on paved and improved trails. Because these are commercial enterprises, fees are charged.

As you approach Massanutten Mountain and enter George Washington National Forest, you can clearly see the break in the ridge at New Market Gap, which you will soon cross. At the top of the ridge is a Forest Service center with exhibits. Several trailheads lead off from the center.

The road descends to New Market to a stop sign at US 11. The main drive turns right (north) on US 11.

To the left (south) on US 11/211 are side trips to New Market Battlefield Historical Park and Endless Caverns. In 1864, Confederate General John Breckinridge, outnumbered two to one, defeated Union troops in one of the most dramatic battles of the Civil War. Some 257 cadets from Virginia Military Institute (VMI) participated, and 10 cadets were killed. The battlefield park details this story. The facilities, operated privately by VMI, include battlefield tours and perhaps the finest Civil War museum in the state.

To visit the battlefield and museum, go left (south) on US 11/211 for two blocks and then turn right on US 211. Cross I-81 and take the first right to the park. The entrance is well marked. To return to the drive, turn left on 211 as you leave the park and turn left (north) on US 11.

The road sweeps in gentle curves toward New Market Gap.

To visit Endless Caverns, drive south on US 11 for about 3 miles. Turn left at the well-marked turnoff. A beautiful cave, Endless Caverns was developed into a tourist attraction in the 1880s to compete with Luray Caverns, but it never achieved that cave's popularity. After visiting the cave, turn right on US 11 to New Market to rejoin the tour.

U.S. Highway 11, the main route up and down the valley, parallels high-speed I-81. As you head north from New Market, a flat-topped ridge appears on your left with the broad ridge of Massanutten Mountain behind it.

About 4 miles from New Market, turn left at the "Covered Bridge" sign on VA 720. The bridge lies about half a mile from the highway down a tree-shaded road. The Meem's Bottom Bridge, built in 1892, spans the North Fork of the Shenandoah River and is the only covered bridge in the state open to vehicular traffic. It is about 200 feet long. There are a few parking spaces just before the bridge. If you drive through this one-lane truss bridge, continue on the dirt road for about a quarter of a mile where you can easily turn around. When you return to US 11, turn left to continue the drive.

In about 5 miles you pass the entrance to Shenandoah Caverns, another popular tourist stop. This cave features an elevator ride to the cavern floor.

The winding drive passes by the small towns of Mount Jackson, Edinburg, and Woodstock. Low hills and occasional views of the river add variety. Mount Jackson is the gateway to the Shenandoah Valley Music Festival, held each summer at Orkney Springs, about 15 miles west of Mount Jackson. The festival features a varied program from classical to western to light pops.

At Woodstock the road skirts the well-kept grounds of the Massanutten Military Academy.

You reach Strasburg again about 30 miles from New Market. Follow US 11 through town, crossing VA 55.

A few miles north of Strasburg, before reaching Middleton, you see to your left the entrance to Belle Grove Plantation. Designed in part by Thomas Jefferson, this restored, historic mansion was the honeymoon site for James and Dolley Madison, and is now the home of the Virginia Quilt Museum.

The area was also the scene of the Battle of Cedar Creek, the last major Civil War battle of the Shenandoah Valley. More than 6,000 soldiers died here when Union General Philip Sheridan narrowly defeated Confederate General Jubal Early. The actual battlefield extended from Strasburg almost to Middleton. Numerous roadside markers point out places and describe events of the Civil War.

On the right side of US 11 across from Belle Grove is the Cedar Creek Battlefield Foundation, which devotes itself to preserving and restoring the battlefield. The U.S. Congress recently authorized establishment of a Shenandoah Valley National Battlefield Park, which is being funded both publicly and privately. Plans are actively underway for acquisitions of land and for restoration in several places, including Cedar Creek.

The drive continues on US 11 to end where you began in Winchester.

Meem's Bottom Bridge, one of the few covered bridges in the state, spans the North Fork of the Shenandoah River.

2

Leesburg Loop
Hunt Country and the Snickersville Pike

General description: This 50-mile loop drive passes through the hilly hunt country west and north of Leesburg in the northern tip of the state. This is a varied area of scenic and historical interest with many large estates, horse farms, open fields, small towns and villages, and the historic town of Leesburg.
Special attractions: Of special interest is Whites Ferry across the Potomac, and the historic town of Waterford. The up-and-down hills of the Snickersville Turnpike provide a scenic and memorable driving experience, and the nine-teenth-century mansion and grounds at Oatlands will give you a glimpse of how the privileged lived in colonial days.
Location: The drive begins and ends in Leesburg in north-central Virginia. Leesburg is easily reached in about an hour from Washington, D.C., via the Dulles Toll Road extension or Virginia Highway 7.
Drive route numbers: U.S. Highways 15, Business 15, and 50; Virginia Highways 655, 7, 665, 672, 673, 690, 9, and 734.
Travel season: The drive can be made at any time of the year. Most of the attractions are busiest—and have the most activities—during the warmer months; they may have reduced hours or limited operations from late October through May. The crafts festival in Waterford the first week in October attracts large crowds.
Camping: Not available.
Services: Gasoline, motels, hotels, and restaurants are abundant in Leesburg; gasoline and restaurants can be found in all towns along the drive.
Nearby attractions: Leesburg is less than an hour from Washington, D.C., and all the attractions of the nation's capital. Drive 3, George Washington Parkway, provides views across the Potomac of many of the Washington sights.

 # The Drive

Horses, hounds, and hunting have been the traditional trademarks of the rolling Piedmont area around Leesburg since colonial days. Just a short distance from Washington, D.C., its bucolic nature has been a magnet for many who want to dwell in the country but whose business requires them to be near the hustle and bustle of the nation's capital.

On this 50-mile loop drive you'll pass many large mansions with manicured lawns, long wooden fences, and horse barns and trailers. The hills, vales, curves, and woods that attract fox hunters (and sometimes attract foxes) pass through sleepy villages, often through open country with distant views of gentle peaks and ridges.

You'll view (and can ride on) the only operating ferry on the Potomac, drive through the historic village of Waterford, restored to look as it did 150 years ago, ride up and down the hilly Snickersville Turnpike, and tour the restored plantation and gardens of Oatlands.

Much of the drive is over narrow country roads that may be poorly marked, so check route numbers carefully on these back roads, particularly at intersections.

The drive begins and ends in historic Leesburg. Originally known as George Town, the town broke ties with England in 1758 and took the name Leesburg in honor of Virginia's prestigious family. Today its narrow downtown streets are lined with colonial-style, tony shops and restaurants.

Although the town still retains its rural character, it is beginning to feel the press of suburbia. It is an easy commute from Leesburg to Dulles Airport and the high-tech centers of Fairfax County, and less than an hour's drive to downtown Washington. This influx of commuters is shown by the new townhouses, condos, and apartment complexes that have sprung up in several places.

While in town you may want to visit Ball's Bluff Regional Park, which describes the retreat of Union soldiers across the Potomac in a small battle fought here in 1861. North of town is the columned mansion at Morven Park, home to several nineteenth-century Virginia governors. On the grounds are extensive boxwood gardens and, if you want to learn more about fox hunting history, the Museum of Hounds and Hunting. To learn more about the city's history, visit the Loudoun Museum.

The actual drive begins with a short side trip to Whites Ferry. Head north from Leesburg on either US 15 or Business 15. The two roads join just north of town to become US 15. Follow US 15 north for about a mile to the "Ferry" sign and turn right onto VA 655.

Virginia 655 leads directly to the shores of the Potomac River. It then turns sharply to the left along the river bank on a tree-shaded road for about 0.5 mile to Whites Ferry, the only car ferry across the Potomac. There are a few parking spaces near the ferry landing.

A ferry has run from this spot since the early 1800s. The current boat, named for the Confederate General Jubal A. Early, was installed in 1988 and can carry about 15 cars; commuter traffic in the morning and evening often fills the vessel to capacity. If you have time, you can ride the ferry over and back as a pedestrian for a nominal sum.

Drive 2: Leesburg Loop
Hunt Country and the Snickersville Pike

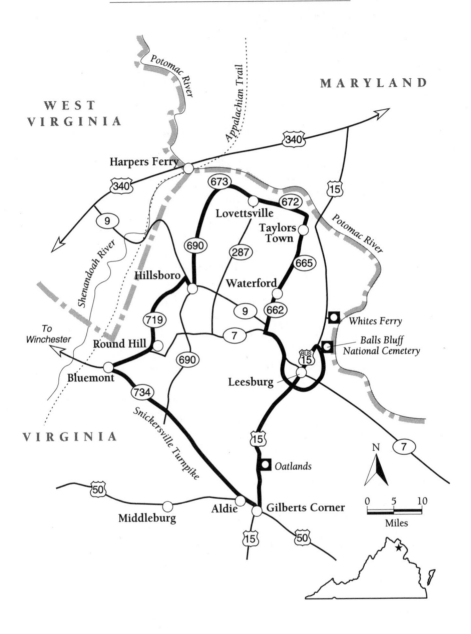

The General Jubal A. Early docks on the Virginia side of the Potomac River across from Whites Ferry, Maryland.

The ferryboat is run by a diesel engine that pulls the boat along a cable stretched across the river. The town of Whites Ferry is actually in Maryland, about 1,000 feet away across the roily Potomac.

When you leave to continue the drive, follow VA 655 back to US 15 and turn left, retracing your route to Leesburg. You can take either Business 15 (shorter but more congested) through Leesburg or US 15 (longer but faster) around town to VA 7. Whatever route you take, turn right (west) onto VA 7.

Follow VA 7 west a few miles to VA 9. Go less than 0.5 mile on VA 9 and turn right (toward Waterford) onto VA 662. This curvy Virginia byway passes numerous cattle and horse farms and open fields.

When you arrive in Waterford, you'll think you have stepped back 100 years in time as you drive past several blocks of lovingly restored, two- and three-story colonial and federal houses. Settled by Quakers in 1733, the town became a thriving crafts and farming community. During the Civil War, Confederate harassment led many townspeople to support Union troops, despite the traditional Quaker belief in nonviolence. This led to widespread destruction of the town by both sides.

The town languished until the 1940s when the Waterford Foundation began sponsoring an annual crafts fair. The success of this fair resulted in extensive renovations and restorations. Today the fair, held the first week-end in October, attracts some 150 craftspeople. In addition, there are public tours of a dozen or more restored homes along its tree-shaded streets. The entire village is listed as a National Historic Landmark.

From Waterford, follow VA 665, Royalton Road, north. The countryside here is wilder and less settled, with more woods and unused fields. You pass the old general store in Taylorstown and cross Catoctin Creek, a state scenic creek.

At the stop sign north of Taylorstown, turn left onto VA 672, Lovettsville Road. The narrow road twists and turns its way toward Lovettsville. Bear right on VA 673. Just before Lovettsville, you pass the First German Reformed Church site and cemetery dating back to 1748. The church is gone, but the cemetery contains several rough rock headstones with crudely carved names and dates more than 200 years old.

At the stop sign in Lovettsville, cross VA 287 and continue straight ahead on VA 673. About 2 miles out of town, turn right onto VA 690, also known as Mountain Road.

The Appalachian Trail follows the top of the ridge on the low hills to the right, which also marks the Virginia–West Virginia boundary. When West Virginia seceded from Virginia and joined the Union in 1863, the boundary in this area was set as the watershed divide between the Potomac (on this side of the ridge) and the Shenandoah (on the other side of the ridge). This sounds simple, but the two states did not agree on an exact boundary line until 1997 when satellite surveys finally helped settle the dispute. This was

A patriotic banner adds a touch of class to a restored building in historic Waterford.

a relief to many residents, who until then were not sure what state they were living in (and should pay taxes to).

At the stop sign in Hillsboro, turn right on VA 9. A former mill town, Hillsboro has several blocks of beautiful, 100-year-old stone houses lining both sides of the road. The town is the birthplace of Susan Koerner Wright, mother of airplane inventors Wilbur and Orville. Follow VA 9 through town.

On the other side of Hillsboro, turn left onto VA 719, Woodgrove Road. Follow this wooded country lane for about 7 miles to Round Hill. Turn right in Round Hill onto VA Business 7, and turn right again in about 0.5 mile when the drive joins the main VA 7, a four-lane highway.

Virginia 7 climbs a long hill with several vistas to your left. After 4 miles, turn left onto VA 734 towards Bluemont. You are entering the Snickersville Turnpike, a Virginia byway. This narrow, two-lane road makes several hairpin turns and heads downhill like a runaway roller coaster. You soon pass by the stately stone houses and Snickersville Country Store in the little town of Bluemont and cross a one-lane bridge.

After several miles of mostly downhill travel, the landscape levels out, but the sharp curves continue. Horse farms and executive-type mansions are intermixed with farmland; the predominant crops in season are hay, corn, and soybeans. To the left you pass the entrance to Willowcroft Farm Vineyards. Like most of the more than 40 wineries in the state, Willowcroft Farm provides tours and tasting rooms.

Virginia 734 and the Snickersville Turnpike end at US 50. The main drive turns left (east) on US 50.

For a side trip to Middleburg, a popular weekend destination from the D.C. suburbs, turn right on US 50 and drive about 5 miles to the town. This historic town is known for its upscale shops, inns, and restaurants. The oldest winery in the state, the Piedmont Vineyards and Winery, is nearby, as are the Meredyth Vineyard and Swedenburg Estates Vineyard. When you are ready to leave Middleburg, turn around and drive east on US 50 to continue with the main drive.

Back on US 50 you soon pass through Aldie, known for its antique shops and old mill. The Aldie Mill is being restored, including its original millstone hoist. Just past the mill the drive crosses a historic, narrow, two-lane stone bridge built during colonial days. The bridge is the center of a controversy between preservationists who hope to save it and commuters who see it as a dangerous bottleneck.

At the stop sign in Gilbert's Corner a mile past Aldie, turn left onto US 15 and head back toward Leesburg. Although it's a two-lane road, US 15 is a major highway and traffic can be heavy. Most of the route follows a discontinuous ridge with downhill views to the right of open fields, farms, and wooded estates.

Just past Goose Creek you come to the long, tree-shaded entranceway to Oatlands, an expansive colonial mansion and gardens. Turn right up the drive to visit, or continue on US 50 for 6 miles to Leesburg.

Oatlands is part of an 11,500-acre tract purchased by the Carter family from Lord Fairfax. In 1804 George Carter built his country house on the estate. The house served as a boarding house during the Civil War; like so many others in Virginia, the estate fell into disrepair after the conflict. It was reclaimed and restored by William Corcoran Eustis, grandson of the founder of the Corcoran Art Gallery in Washington, D.C.

In addition to the three-story mansion with its stately columns and spacious wings, Oatlands contains extensive terraced gardens with shady boxwood tunnels, wisteria walkways, and herb plantings. The mansion contains a mix of American and European furnishings, including some dessert plates that belonged to George Washington. Other interesting features are the octagonal drawing room—very stylish in the early 1800s—and elaborate plasterwork in several rooms.

When you leave Oatlands, turn right on US 50. In a few miles the condos and developments south of Leesburg appear, and in 6 miles you reach Leesburg, the beginning and end of the drive.

3

George Washington Memorial Parkway

Capital Views

General description: This 25-mile national parkway follows the shoreline of the Potomac River upstream from Mount Vernon, through historic Alexandria, past the skyline of Washington, D.C., with dramatic views of many monuments and bridges of the nation's capital, and through the gorge of the upper Potomac to the end of the parkway at Interstate 495, the Capital Beltway. Visitors to Washington can easily make this drive in a few hours.

Special attractions: George Washington's home at Mount Vernon; open stretches of the lower Potomac; Old Town Alexandria; close-ups of takeoffs and landings at Reagan National Airport; views of the Washington, D.C., skyline, including the Washington Monument, the Lincoln Memorial, and the Capitol; and the gorge of the upper Potomac.

Location: The drive, which is across the Potomac River from Washington, D.C., in northern Virginia, starts at Mount Vernon, about 15 miles south of Washington. You can also join the ride in mid-route from Washington by crossing the Potomac on one of the many bridges and following signs to the parkway.

Drive route numbers: Most of the drive follows the George Washington Memorial Parkway, which does not have a route number. The parkway becomes Washington Street (Virginia Highway 400) as you cross Old Town Alexandria. Interstate 495 and Virginia Highways 123 and 193 are used at the north end of the drive to reverse direction.

Travel season: Avoid rush hour. The time of day is more important than the time of year. The parkway is a major commuter route in both directions morning and evening. The best views of the Washington skyline are in winter when leaves are off the trees. Spring and fall are best for flowering plants and trees. However, except for occasional winter snowstorms, the ride can be made any time. An after-dark ride provides an enthralling and different view of the Washington skyline.

Services: Motels, hotels, restaurants, gasoline, and shopping malls are available in abundance in Alexandria and Washington, D.C.

Nearby attractions: All of the monuments and buildings of the nation's capital are nearby, including the U.S. Capitol, the National Mall, the Lincoln and Jefferson Memorials, the Washington Monument, and the Vietnam Memorial. The art, space, zoo, natural history, and other museums of the Smithsonian Institution are also in Washington, D.C., just across the Potomac.

Drive 3: George Washington Memorial Parkway
Capital Views

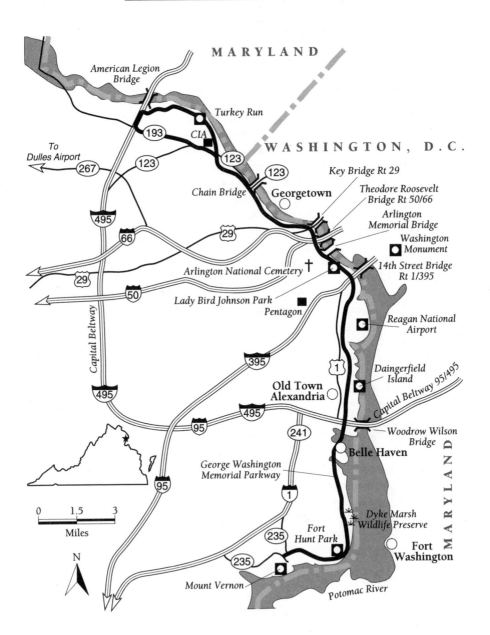

MARYLAND

American Legion Bridge

Turkey Run

193

CIA

123

To Dulles Airport

267

123

123

WASHINGTON, D.C.

Key Bridge Rt 29

Chain Bridge

Georgetown

Theodore Roosevelt Bridge Rt 50/66

Arlington Memorial Bridge

Washington Monument

14th Street Bridge Rt 1/395

495

66

29

Arlington National Cemetery

50

29

Lady Bird Johnson Park

Pentagon

Reagan National Airport

Daingerfield Island

Capital Beltway 95/495

395

1

Capital Beltway

Old Town Alexandria

495

95

495

241

Woodrow Wilson Bridge

George Washington Memorial Parkway

Belle Haven

95

1

MARYLAND

Dyke Marsh Wildlife Preserve

Fort Washington

Fort Hunt Park

235

0 1.5 3

Miles

N

235

Mount Vernon

Potomac River

 # The Drive

Washington, D.C., the capital of the United States, is separated from Virginia by the Potomac River. The George Washington Memorial Parkway parallels the Potomac for 25 miles, from George Washington's home at Mount Vernon 15 miles south of Washington, to I-495 (the Capital Beltway) 10 miles north of the U.S. Capitol. The parkway is a component of National Capital Parks administered by the National Park Service.

The drive begins at Mount Vernon, George Washington's home and estate. From there, you follow the winding shore of the Potomac upstream toward Washington. The drive passes through landscaped hardwoods with many views of the wide estuary. You pass a restored colonial fort across the Potomac in Maryland that once guarded the river. Turnouts and overlooks allow you to visit marinas and a wildlife preserve known for its variety of shore and wading birds. You then pass through Old Town Alexandria, known for its shops and historic buildings.

The parkway continues on the other side of Alexandria. It winds past Reagan National Airport as the Washington skyline comes into view. You pass by the Washington Monument and Lincoln Memorial, and drive under Memorial Bridge. The Potomac narrows to a gorge as you pass the Key Bridge and Georgetown. The drive ends at I-495, the Capital Beltway north of Washington, where you can reverse direction and return south on the parkway, or drive away on the Beltway.

Although the drive is described from south to north (that is, starting at Mount Vernon) it can be picked up at many points along the route. This can be convenient for visitors to Washington, D.C., who can cross one of the several bridges to Virginia and join the drive in the middle. If you do this, go north (to your right as you leave the District, but follow the signs), drive along the parkway to I-495, and follow instructions to reverse directions and head south.

The reason for this is that north of Alexandria the parkway is primarily a divided highway and most of the overlooks and turnoffs toward the Potomac can be made only from the northbound lanes—you will not be able to access the overlooks if you are going south. In addition, the views of the Potomac gorge are better as you head north. The southbound lanes are often set back away from the river; it is a pretty drive, but you do not have as good a view of the river's rocky gorge.

Reversing directions is easy at the Mount Vernon end. The parkway terminates in a broad circle, or you can pull into the Mount Vernon parking area to reverse direction.

Scenic it may be, but this drive becomes a bumper-to-bumper commuter route in both directions every workday morning and evening. Traffic moves fast (when it isn't gridlocked), and it is heavy because the parkway is one of the few north-south highways in the metropolitan area. Avoid taking this drive workdays between 7:00 to 9:30 A.M. and 3:30 to 6:30 P.M.

Mount Vernon, the beginning of the drive, was George Washington's primary home and estate from 1754 until his death in 1799. Washington considered himself to be a farmer, although the duties of war and a young country kept him away from his beloved home for much of this time. After his death, Mount Vernon passed out of family control and lay neglected for many years. In 1858 the Mount Vernon Ladies' Association, a group formed by women to restore the estate, bought the rundown building and grounds for $200,000, an enormous sum for those days. Through their efforts at fundraising, and with the help of Washington's detailed notes and writings, it has been restored to reflect his life as a gentleman farmer and landowner. Guided tours today show the mansion, Washington's tomb, 12 outbuildings, and museums to give a detailed view of early colonial life, including the lives and work of the many slaves who operated and maintained the estate.

The drive from Mount Vernon follows the four-lane parkway past hardwood groves and graceful concrete bridges. This section of the parkway was carefully planned and built in the 1930s to be as scenic as possible, modeled after the scenic parkways then being constructed outside New York City.

You quickly approach the Potomac River, a mile-wide, tidewater estuary at this point. A scenic turnout at Riverside Park has picnic tables and gives access to the riverside trail and bike path that parallel the parkway. A

Walkers, bikers, and sightseers gaze across the Potomac River at the Washington Monument and the dome-shaped Jefferson Memorial.

mile farther on are the batteries at Fort Hunt Park. Across the river in Maryland lies restored Fort Washington with its high masonry walls. These fortifications were built to protect the bustling, upriver colonial ports of Alexandria and Georgetown. However, Fort Washington was destroyed in the War of 1812 and rebuilt in 1814.

The Belle Haven Marina turnout a few miles farther on is a popular spot for weekend boaters to put their craft in the river. The marina provides excellent views of the wide Potomac downriver. Birders (and others) will want to visit the trail through the estuary wetland of Dyke Marsh Wildlife Preserve. The brackish nature of the river (part fresh, part salt) attracts many wading birds, both freshwater and shore birds—more than 250 species.

Continue on the parkway across the Capital Beltway (here called I-95/I-495) and enter Alexandria on Washington Street, VA 400. Alexandria, founded in 1749, was a major colonial port. You can temporarily leave the drive and follow signs to visit Old Town Alexandria with its numerous, restored, colonial and federal homes, or tour its many historic buildings such as Gadsby's Tavern, Carlyle House, and the boyhood home of Robert E. Lee.

The arts are not neglected here; the Torpedo Factory Art Center, which manufactured munitions for two world wars, is now the home of the urban Alexandria Archeology Museum plus displays by more than 175 working artists, potters, sculptors, and other craftspeople who welcome the public to view their work. Shops and walks along the river have replaced the colonial trading ships, although river tours of Alexandria and the Washington skyline are available in modern vessels.

To continue on the parkway, stay on Washington Street. The parkway resumes as a four-lane, divided road just north of Alexandria. The turnoff at Daingerfield Island gives you another opportunity to walk along the river or watch birds.

The drive curves away from the river as you pass the runways of Reagan National Airport on the right. As you drive by, you will see the modernistic new control tower and the numerous "Jeffersonian domes" of the terminal that opened in 1997. The airport, known for years as National Airport or Washington National Airport, was officially named the Ronald Reagan National Airport by Congress in 1998.

Just past the airport, the skyline of Washington lies straight ahead. If you like watching planes land and take off, turn right just after the airport into the picnic area at Gravelly Point. This spit of land is separated from the main airport runway by a few hundred feet of water. Jets roar by just overhead as numerous airplane watchers crane their necks skyward. Depending on the wind and runway use, you may see (and hear), close up, takeoffs or landings.

Soon you cross I-95/I-395 and pass several auto and railroad bridges. The city of Washington lies just across what is here a much narrower river.

Easily recognized are the Jefferson Memorial (another Jeffersonian dome) and the columns of the Lincoln Memorial. Above all stands the Washington Monument; behind it in the distance are the Mall and the Capitol. To the left, in Virginia, is the huge Pentagon Building, headquarters for the Department of Defense, but because you see only one or two sides at a time, you can't tell it is a five-sided building.

For an unhurried view, pull off at Lady Bird Johnson Park, less than 0.5 mile past the I-95/I-395 bridges. The marina is directly across the Potomac from the Tidal Basin, known for its hundreds of cherry trees that bloom each spring.

Dominating the scene at Lady Bird Johnson Park is the 555.5-foot spire of the Washington Monument across the Potomac, an icon of the city and the country as well known as the Capitol itself. Construction began on the monument in 1848 after a nationwide drive for funds. In 1854, when the monument was 150 feet tall, money ran out and work stopped. Construction did not resume for 25 years until President Grant allocated funds. Because slightly darker marble from a different quarry was used to continue construction, a line on the monument 150 feet up clearly delineates the two construction periods. When the monument was first opened, the elevator was considered unsafe, so women and children were required to walk up the stairs to the observation tower; men, however, could ride.

Another public fundraising drive netted more than $5 million for a monumental face-lifting and refurbishing. Begun in 1997, this job includes replacing the elevator, refurbishing the observation booth, pointing up stone in the monument, and a thorough housecleaning. If you take this drive before the year 2001, you will probably see the monument enclosed in its "see-through" scaffolding erected for the renovation.

From Lady Bird Johnson Park, the drive sweeps under Arlington Memorial Bridge. This bridge leads across the Potomac to the Lincoln Memorial. From the drive you can easily see the back of the Lincoln Memorial with its many columns of white marble, fashioned after the ancient Greek Parthenon.

Arlington National Cemetery lies to your left in Virginia. (Follow signs before the Memorial Bridge to visit the cemetery.) Well-known sites in Arlington Cemetery include the eternal light at the grave of President John F. Kennedy, the Tombs of the Unknowns, and the U.S. Marine Corps Memorial, a bronze statue of the famous World War II photograph showing marines raising the flag at Iwo Jima. President Lincoln established the cemetery in 1864 to bury the many severely wounded Civil War soldiers who lay dying in a nearby Arlington tent hospital. Today representatives of those killed in all American wars are buried here, from the American Revolution to Vietnam to the Persian Gulf.

Continuing on the drive, you pass under the Theodore Roosevelt Memorial Bridge with views of the green woods of Theodore Roosevelt Island in the Potomac. A parking lot past the bridge gives access to a footbridge to the island, which contains wooded trails and a statue of President Roosevelt.

The Potomac narrows. The flat, open vistas are replaced by tree-covered slopes as you drive under the graceful arches of the Key Bridge, a memorial to Francis Scott Key, author of the Star Spangled Banner. Across the river lies Georgetown, known for its historic houses and upscale shopping.

Now a part of Washington, Georgetown in colonial days was one of the busiest ports in the nation. Small rapids in the river, which you may not be able to see from the drive, mark the head of navigation, known as the Fall Line, and the end of the tidewater Potomac. It also marks the boundary between the unconsolidated sands and sediments of the coastal plain that you have been driving on and the harder, older crystalline rocks to the north.

The towers and spires you see are part of Georgetown University. Founded in 1789 as the first Catholic university in the country, the school is known today for its prestigious international affairs programs.

The drive climbs above the river, which here is narrow and rocky and lies in a distinct gorge. Several overlooks allow you to gaze down on the water and the gorge's steep far side. Soon you leave the river and drive past thick woods and steep slopes on both sides of the road.

It's hard to believe the Potomac River can look so tranquil and unspoiled just a few miles north of downtown Washington, D.C.

The drive crosses under Chain Bridge and continues through woods. For a view of the rapids in this part of the river, turn into the picnic grounds at the Turkey Run Recreation Area. You may want to reflect on how much the river has changed from the broad, tidewater estuary at the beginning of the drive.

As you approach I-495, the Capital Beltway, signs announce the end of the George Washington Parkway. To head north to Maryland (toward Baltimore), bear right and follow the signs; to head south (toward Richmond), bear left.

To reverse direction and return to the parkway heading south, go south on the Beltway (toward Richmond) for 0.8 mile and take Exit 13, VA 193 (Georgetown Pike). Turn left on VA 193, a state-designated scenic highway, and cross over I-495. This two-lane, curvy road takes you past million-dollar executive mansions and several groves of tall hardwoods, some more than a century old.

Follow VA 193 about 3 miles to the light at VA 123, the Dolley Madison Highway. Turn left on VA 123. Just after the turn a sign points to the headquarters of the CIA on the left. For years the location and even the existence of the Central Intelligence Agency was classified, so no sign was permitted at the entrance. The intersection with the George Washington Memorial Parkway is about a block past CIA headquarters. Turn right (toward Alexandria) onto the George Washington Parkway. You are now heading south on the parkway just above Chain Bridge.

4

Piedmont–Blue Ridge Vistas
Warrenton to Charlottesville

General description: Beginning at Warrenton, this 55-mile drive takes you past the rolling hills of the Piedmont horse country to imposing views of the Blue Ridge Mountains and Shenandoah National Park. The drive then winds through the foothills of the Blue Ridge with constant views of the ridgeline through several picturesque small towns. The drive ends at the outskirts of Charlottesville.

Special attractions: Rolling hills of Piedmont area, extended scenic vistas of the Blue Ridge Mountains, including Old Rag and the F.T. Valley. Side trips to historic Washington, Virginia, landslides from 1995 floods, Montpelier, and the Barboursville Ruins.

Location: North-central Virginia. Warrenton is about 50 miles west of Washington, D.C., via Interstate 66 and U.S. Highway 29.

Drive route numbers: U.S. Highways 211, 522, and 29; Virginia Highways 231 and 20. The landslide side trip uses US 29 and VA 230 and 622.

Travel season: All year long, although roads may be temporarily closed during occasional heavy winter snows. Winter also brings the clearest days for exceptional views of the mountains and without intervening vegetation. Spring is the best time for flowering trees and shrubs. Hot, hazy summer days can obscure views of the mountains. Fall leaf colors can be outstanding, but this attracts large numbers of visitors.

Camping: Available in several campgrounds in Shenandoah National Park. These often are filled on summer weekends. Check with the park for dates and availability.

Services: Gasoline, motels, and restaurants are available in Warrenton and Charlottesville. Numerous gas stations and restaurants can be found in the small towns along the route.

Nearby attractions: Monticello, Charlottesville, Montpelier, Shenandoah National Park, Skyline Drive (Drive 5) and Blue Ridge Parkway North (Drive 6).

 The Drive

On this 55-mile drive you cross rolling Piedmont country with distant views of the Blue Ridge Mountains. The countryside alternates between hardwood forest and open fields of cattle and hay. Gradually you approach the mountains, and then drive along the base of the Blue Ridge for 30 miles

Drive 4: Piedmont–Blue Ridge Vistas
Warrenton to Charlottesville

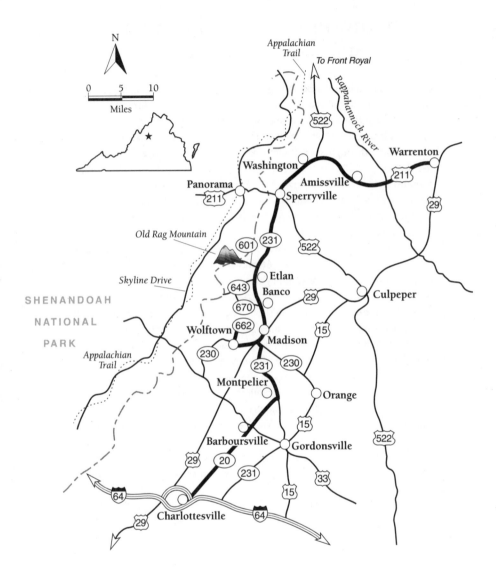

It's easy to balance your budget with rates like these.

If you're looking for great hotel values in the Washington, D.C. area, choose one of our great hotels. You'll get features like a 100% Satisfaction Guarantee, free morning newspapers, free local calls, the *Guest Privileges*® frequent traveler program and free continental breakfast.* Plus, we offer a special discount for Washington, D.C. visitors, just **call the toll-free number of the brand of your choice and ask for the L-VALUE rate.**

 Use Every Advantage.℠ At over 150 locations in 15 countries, Clarion offers amenities and services like our unique Clarion Class Business Rooms, a BizNet Center, complete meeting facilities, full-service restaurants, and more. **1-800-CLARION®**

 HOW TO RUN A HOTEL.℠ For 60 years, Quality Inns, Hotels and Suites have provided great value and a comfortable guest experience. Today, Quality Sleeper mattresses by Serta® in-room Maxwell House coffee and free local calls are some of the reasons guests trust Quality to make everything just right. **1-800-228-5151**

 Room to be yourself.℠ Separate areas for you to live, work and sleep. Complimentary breakfast buffet plus in-room refrigerator, coffee maker and microwave. All designed to give you more room to be yourself. **1-800-517-4000**

 It's more than a room. It's Comfort.℠ Enjoy extra amenities when you stay at Comfort Inn. Free continental breakfast, a pool or exercise facilities, 100% satisfaction guarantee and over 1200 locations throughout the U.S. **1-800-228-5150**

 In a class by itself.℠ Get what you came for – a good night's sleep. Sleep Inn and Sleep Inn & Suites are smartly designed, warmly decorated, and staffed with friendly people whose only task is to see that you have a pleasant stay. A promise backed by our 100% Satisfaction Guarantee. **1-800-SLEEP-INN®**

*Amenities vary by brand.

along a state scenic road with many spectacular views. Optional side trips allow you to visit a town surveyed by George Washington, a mountain scarred by landslides, a mansion and plantation that belonged to James Madison, and the remains of a mansion designed by Thomas Jefferson.

The drive begins in Warrenton, county seat of Fauquier County. The town began as a trading post in the 1700s, and until late in that century it was considered to be the western frontier of English civilization in the Virginia colony. Several old buildings are open to the public, including the Old Court House and Old Jail Museum which once sported a three-person gallows. During the Civil War, Warrenton was headquarters for the Gray Ghosts, a vigilante group led by Confederate Colonel John Mosby. Mosby, whose group was also known as Mosby's Raiders, is buried in a nearby cemetery along with 600 other Confederate soldiers.

The drive heads west on four-lane US 211 through open, gentle hills of the Fauquier County horse country. Virginia likes to name its highways after favorite sons, and calls US 211 the Lee Highway. On non-hazy days the Blue Ridge Mountains appear on the distant horizon. You pass numerous large mansions and well-kept fields, with grazing horses and cattle. You may even see several practice rings with jumps and bars.

The road descends to cross the Rappahannock River, a designated state scenic river. About 10 miles from Warrenton on the left, just past the small town of Amissville, are the grapevines of the Gray Ghost Vineyard, the first of several wineries along this drive. Although it is a relatively small winery, the Gray Ghost wines have won numerous prizes. Viniculture has been a Virginia industry since colonial days. Most wineries, including the Gray Ghost, welcome visitors and provide tasting rooms and guided tours. Highway signs direct you to numerous wineries off the main route.

Several long hills provide panoramic views of the mountains, which present an unbroken, undulating line of peaks stretching left and right as far as you can see. The mountains get their name "Blue Ridge" from their typical hazy blue appearance most of the year.

Continue straight on US 211 where it joins US 522 south. To the right, US 522 goes to Front Royal, the northern entrance of Shenandoah National Park and the starting point for Skyline Drive (Drive 5).

The road, now US 211/522, makes a series of lazy S-turns that bring you closer to and parallel with the mountains. In a few minutes you pass US Business 211 on the right, which leads to the town of Washington, county seat of Rappahannock County. There are more than 25 towns named "Washington" in the United States (plus Washington state and the federal city, of course) but Washington, Virginia, claims to be the first Washington of all. It is sometimes known as "Little Washington" to distinguish it from the somewhat larger federal seat of government 70 miles to the east.

The town was laid out and surveyed by George Washington in 1747 when the future president was 17 years old. This project brought Washington's first paid remuneration; he received two pounds, three shillings. The town is also the unlikely home of the only five-star restaurant in the United States, the Inn at Little Washington, renowned for chef Patrick O'Connell's signature dishes. (The Inn is expensive, and reservations are strongly recommended.) The Inn is located on the right at the only stop sign in town. Also in town are several small craft shops and an art gallery. You can follow Business 211 through the town and back to the main highway without retracing your route.

Back on US 211/522, turn right. The mountains and Shenandoah National Park are on your right, with rounded peaks 2,000 to 3,000 feet above you. In places, the wooded foothills of mixed hardwood extend down almost to the highway; in other places, broad valleys, known locally as hollows, provide open vistas to the distant peaks.

At Sperryville, just after the four-lane highway ends, turn left and follow US 522 where it branches off from US 211. U.S. Highway 211 continues straight ahead 2 miles to a crafts and glass-blowing center before it climbs up the mountain to intersect with Drive 5, Skyline Drive, at Panorama. Cross the river and turn left again in the middle of Sperryville on US 522.

Sperryville is in the heart of apple country, and is known for its Apple Festival held each October at the peak of the fall leaf season. The quaint look of the town is enhanced by many buildings preserved to look much as they did in the 1920s. It is also a craft and art center with numerous shops.

Follow US 522 about a mile to the intersection with VA 231. Turn right on VA 231, a Virginia Scenic Byway. For several miles this winding road follows the F. T. Valley, snuggled between the Blue Ridge Mountains on the right and the hills of the Piedmont on the left. The valley gets its name from Francis Thornton, an early landowner, who notched his initials on trees to mark the way; travelers learned to follow the F. T. Trail.

The mountains are beautiful year-round, with each season having special merits. In summer, verdant slopes stretch from the foothills to the highest summits. As the shortening days of autumn approach, the countryside is bathed in a thousand shades of orange, yellow, brown, and red as the leaves turn. Winter days are often the clearest. The lower hills look gray and black, contrasting with the higher peaks that are often coated with snow. Occasional snowstorms at lower elevations turn the landscape into a stark contrast of black and white. In spring, the hillsides turn yellow and then green as spring creeps up the mountainsides day by day.

About 3 miles from Sperryville is a good view of Old Rag Mountain, a popular destination for hikers in Shenandoah National Park. "Old Rag" is short for Old Raggedy, so named because of several prominent, step-like ledges that give the mountain its distinctive, serrated appearance. The mountain is

Old Rag Mountain is a popular destination for hikers in Shenandoah National Park.

composed of billion-year-old granite—some of the oldest rocks in the Blue Ridge—that was later intruded by lava flows of basalt. Because the basalt, changed by heat and pressure into greenstone, is more resistant to weathering than the granite, the basalt weathers into steep cliffs or ledges to form the stair-like appearance.

Several side roads off VA 231 lead to hiking trails in the park. However, stay on VA 231 for the main drive. Eight miles from Sperryville, VA 601 turns right to lead to the Old Rag trailhead. This trail has become so popular that the National Park Service now limits the number of hikers on busy summer weekends. At Etlan, 10 miles from Sperryville, a right turn on VA 643 takes you to the White Oak Canyon trail, known for its steep canyons and numerous waterfalls.

At Banco, look right at the intersection with VA 670 to see scars of a landslide on the mountain in the distance. Banco may look peaceful as you drive through it today, but on the night of June 27, 1975, the town and road were under several feet of water after more than 23 inches of rain poured down, flooding Banco and most of the other small towns along this route.

Continue on VA 231, crossing the Robinson River on a new bridge, rebuilt since the flood. After passing through the town of Madison, county seat of Madison County, VA 231 turns right to join four-lane US 29. Service stations and restaurants are available along this stretch.

You now have to decide whether to continue on the main drive, or make a 20-mile side trip over rough roads to see a mountain scarred by landslides.

To continue on the main drive, VA 231 turns left in 3 miles, leaving US 29. Turn left here for the main drive and skip the next several paragraphs.

Kirtley Mountain side trip:

For the side trip to see a mountain scarred by slides and other flood damage, stay on US 29 for another mile past where VA 231 turned left, about 4 miles from Madison. Turn right on VA 230. (Do not confuse VA 230 with 231.) This side trip takes you over some rough country roads and adds about 20 miles total to the drive. It is not suitable for trailers.

Follow VA 230 3 miles to Wolftown and turn right on VA 662. You are driving up the small valley of the Rapidan River. This entire valley was covered by water during the June 1975 floods, and the road and bridges have been rebuilt since then.

To the left is an impressive view of the numerous landslides on Kirtley Mountain that occurred the night of the flood. Because the slides removed all vegetation and scoured the soil down to bare bedrock, the scars of the slides stand out even in summer. The rocks, boulders, debris, trees, and vegetation torn loose in the slide areas were deposited downstream, sometimes several miles from their origin.

You can turn around now or follow VA 662 a few more miles past an old post office and then turn around. Just before the post office you pass a debris trail of material dumped by the slide as it reached flatter ground and slowed down. Because much soil was also deposited along with the rocks,

Peaks of the Blue Ridge, some scarred by landslides, rise in the distance.

Pillars, chimneys, and a few brick walls are all that remain of the former mansion at Barboursville Ruins. The original building was designed by Thomas Jefferson for an early Virginia governor.

vegetation is beginning to return. But in winter, the area looks bare and covered with boulders.

After turning around, retrace your steps: Turn left on VA 230 at Wolftown, turn left again at US 29, drive 1 mile on US 29, and turn right on VA 231 to rejoin the main drive.

Back on the main drive:

VA 231 veers away from the mountains into wooded and rolling Piedmont country. There are numerous herds of beef and dairy cattle. About 10 miles from US 29, turn right onto VA 20.

For a side trip to see James Madison's Montpelier, turn left onto VA 20 toward Orange and follow the signs. Montpelier, a 2,700-acre plantation and mansion, was the retirement home of James and Dolley Madison after he completed his second presidential term in 1817 until his death in 1836. The mansion was renovated extensively by later occupants, but has been partially restored to its state during Madison's occupancy. There are extensive gardens and plantings. In nearby Orange is the James Madison Museum which displays furniture and other artifacts of the fourth president's life.

Virginia Highway 20 continues to the right through woods and open country. The Blue Ridge is visible occasionally in the distance to the right. A low, tree-covered ridge parallels the road for several miles. Continue on VA 20 and cross US 33, about 15 miles from US 29.

Just past the intersection with US 33, turn left off VA 20 and follow the signs for a side trip to the Barboursville Ruins. Here are the remains of a mansion Thomas Jefferson designed for James Barbour, governor of Virginia from 1812 to 1814. The building burned in 1884, leaving only the massive brick foundation and walls for today's visitors. The site serves as the backdrop for summer weekend productions of "Shakespeare at the Ruins." The ruins are on the grounds of the Barboursville Winery, which is open for tastings and tours.

Return to VA 20 and turn left. The drive continues through rolling country with several sharp turns past fields of grazing sheep, cattle, and horses. The drive ends where VA 20 crosses US 250 south of Charlottesville, about 14 miles from Barboursville. Turn right on US 250 to go downtown.

Charlottesville has many attractions, including the beautiful grounds of the University of Virginia, and the Ash Lawn-Highland, James Monroe's Virginia home. Nearby is Monticello, Thomas Jefferson's magnificent mansion and gardens. The starting point for the Blue Ridge Parkway North (Drive 6) is about 20 miles west of Charlottesville on US 64.

5
Skyline Drive
Shenandoah National Park

General description: Skyline Drive in Shenandoah National Park winds for 105 miles along the highest crests of the Blue Ridge Mountains. On one side of this crest is the Shenandoah Valley; on the other is the rolling Piedmont area. Numerous scenic turnouts provide views in all directions. The drive can be made in one day, but a more leisurely trip is recommended to let you stop and enjoy more of the features.

Special attractions: Spectacular vistas of mountains, valleys, ridges, and thick hardwood and pine forests. Deer and other wildlife, birds, wildflowers, century-old trees, exhibits, visitor centers, waterfalls, hikes, and trails all add to your understanding and enjoyment.

Location: Northwestern Virginia outside of Front Royal. Front Royal is about 80 miles east of Washington, D.C., via Interstate 66.

Drive route numbers: Skyline Drive. There is no route number.

Travel season: All year. Summer weekends can be crowded; the heaviest visitation is in mid-October during peak leaf season. Winter storms can temporarily close the drive.

Camping: Campgrounds at Mathews Arm, Big Meadows, Lewis Mountain, and Loft Mountain provide a total of about 650 campsites. The Dundo Group Camp is open to organized groups. Advance reservations are accepted for Big Meadows and Dundo. Campgrounds are usually open from April through October, and are often full on summer and fall weekends.

Services: Gasoline, motels, and restaurants are available in Front Royal, Waynesboro, and Charlottesville. Overnight accommodations in the park are at Skyland Lodge, Big Meadows Lodge, and Lewis Mountain cottages. Operations are limited in winter. Gasoline is available at several places.

Nearby attractions: Front Royal, Skyline Caverns, the Shenandoah Valley, Charlottesville, Blue Ridge Parkway.

 The Drive

Skyline Drive and Shenandoah National Park in northwest Virginia are virtually synonymous. Shenandoah National Park is a long and narrow park that straddles the Blue Ridge Mountains, the easternmost and highest range of the Appalachian Mountains. It includes steep mountains, quiet valleys, streams and waterfalls, and green forests. The 196,000-acre park includes 79,000 acres of designated wilderness.

Drive 5: Skyline Drive
Shenandoah National Park

WEST
VIRGINIA

81 66 522

Front Royal
Entrance Station
Front Royal

Dickey Ridge
Visitor Center

340

Indian
Run

522

Mathews Arm

Range
View

Elkwallow

Thornton Gap
Entrance Station

211

Sperryville

New Market 211

Luray

Mary's Rock Tunnel

Stony Man Mountain 4,010 ft.

Skyland

Hemlock Springs

N

Hawksbill Mountain 4,051 ft.

Old Rag Mountain
3,291 ft.

Big Meadows
Campground

Lewis Mountain Campground

Byrd Visitor Center

29

SHENANDOAH
NATIONAL
PARK

Lewis Mountain

Elkton

South River Picnic Area

33

0   5   10

Miles

Swift Run Gap
Entrance Station

33

81

Loft Mountain Campground

Loft Mountain

340

Dundo Group Camp

Appalachian Trail

29

Calf Mountain

250

250

Charlottesville

64

Waynesboro

Rockfish Gap
Entrance Station

Skyline Drive is a 105-mile-long, mountaintop road within Shenandoah National Park that winds along the rolling ridgetops of the Blue Ridge. It provides all visitors with sweeping vistas of the surrounding mountains and valleys.

Shenandoah National Park was authorized by Congress in 1926. Residents who had not already left the mountains were either bought out or were relocated by the government. This forcible eviction created considerable resentment toward the park and the government, a residue of which still exists today in surrounding communities.

Most of the park's facilities were constructed by Civilian Conservation Corps workers in the 1930s, and Skyline Drive was opened in 1939. The area slowly reverted to its natural state so that now, some 50 years later, 100 species of trees cover about 95 percent of the park.

As the area recovered, so did the native animals, such as deer, bear, bobcat, and turkey. About 200 species of birds have been spotted. The updrafts and thermals created by the ridges turn the area into an aerial highway each spring and fall; it is one of the major flyways for migrating birds. Some spotters have seen flocks of more than 20,000 hawks during the fall migration.

A portion of the Appalachian Trail (AT) runs for 101 miles along almost the full length of the park. This famous footpath runs 2,000 miles from Maine to Georgia. The section in the park parallels and crosses Skyline Drive numerous times. It varies in difficulty from easy to strenuous. Over 450 miles of trails of all types spider-web the park; the most popular ones lead to mountain tops or waterfalls. Many radiate from Skyline Drive and are mentioned below. For a more thorough guide to 59 of the most interesting hikes, see *Hiking Shenandoah National Park* by Bert and Jane Gildart (Falcon Publishing, 1998).

You can make the drive at any time of the year, but most facilities are closed in winter. Occasional ice and snowstorms may temporarily close Skyline Drive. Spring can be especially beautiful as wildflowers come into bloom and green creeps up the mountainsides. Fall weekends are the busiest travel times, usually in mid-October as leaf colors reach their maximum. Much of Shenandoah National Park lies beyond Skyline Drive, a wilderness of streams, hollows, and forests. You may want to plan your trip to visit some off-the-road spots.

Remember that this is a national park; all plant and animal life is protected. Collecting of any sort is prohibited. Do not feed deer or other animals. The maximum speed limit is 35 miles per hour. An entrance fee is charged.

The drive begins at the north end of Front Royal about 80 miles from Washington D.C., via Interstate 66. The town gets its name because its large oak trees—known as royal oaks—were cut for masts for sailing ships. A mile north of the park entrance is Skyline Caverns, known for its delicate, needle-like anthodite crystals.

At the entrance station pay your fee and pick up a park brochure. Mileage markers on the west (right) side of the road mark the distance from the northern entrance (mile 0.0) to Rockfish Gap (mile 105.4) at the southern end. These markers make it easy to locate spots of interest.

The road heads uphill through a thick forest. Road cuts reveal numerous outcrops of the Catoctin basalt or greenstone, an extensive series of lava flows that covered the region in late Precambrian time. The geology of the park is complex. For a detailed explanation of the geologic forces that have shaped the park's landscape, see *Geology Along Skyline Drive* by Robert Badger (Falcon Publishing, 1999).

The road curves steadily uphill to the first scenic overlook at mile 2.8, a view of the Shenandoah Valley. The prominent ridge is the northern end of Massanutten Mountain, which bisects the Shenandoah Valley and extends south for about 40 miles. Signal Knob, the prominent high point, was occupied by both sides during the Civil War (at different times) as a lookout post. Drive 1 follows the ridgeline of Massanutten Mountain. The South Fork of the Shenandoah River lies between the park and Massanutten Mountain; the North Fork of the Shenandoah River flows on the far side of the mountain. The two forks meet just north of Front Royal.

At the Dickey Ridge information center, mile 4.6, are exhibits and more views of the Shenandoah Valley. Detailed hiking and other maps are available. The building originally served as a tavern in the 1930s. A popular hang-gliding launch area is nearby.

The first view to the east at Indian Run, mile 10.1, reveals the low mountains of the Piedmont area. Like ripples spreading in a pond, the hills decrease in elevation away from the park, and eventually die out to a gently rolling plain. Washington, D.C., lies beyond the horizon, about 85 miles to the east.

Numerous dead trees are apparent in many places along the drive. The ice storm in January 1998 snapped off so many treetops and branches that much of Skyline Drive was blocked and closed for several weeks. Hurricane Fran in 1996 toppled many trees. Other trees have been killed by huge numbers of gypsy moth caterpillars and their insatiable appetite for leaves, which can denude full-grown trees in a few days.

Another view to the east at about mile 13 has, unfortunately, an inaccurate geologic display. Among its errors, the display shows limestone rocks forming the tops of the ridges of the Valley and Ridge. Actually, the ridges, such as Massanutten Mountain, are formed of resistant sandstone; the valley floors are underlain by limestone, which often contains caves.

The Appalachian Mountains and the Blue Ridge formed about 320 million years ago when the great continental plates of what are now Africa and Europe slowly crashed into ancestral North America. This continental collision first started to fold the existing rocks. But the forces over time were so powerful that the rocks to the east—today's Blue Ridge—broke, or faulted, in what is known as a thrust fault, and slid over the younger rocks to the west—today's Shenandoah Valley. The rocks of the Shenandoah Valley were also thrust faulted over still younger rocks west of them. These huge thrust faults extend for more than 100 miles along the Blue Ridge.

The Range View overlook at mile 17.1 is aptly named. In one direction lies the irregular, craggy crest of the Blue Ridge; in the other, across the Shenandoah Valley, are the parallel ridge lines of the Valley and Ridge province.

More than 200 species of birds have been reported in the park. Crests and ridges provide updrafts for soaring birds, such as the ubiquitous turkey vulture and numerous hawks and falcons.

The turnoff for the Mathews Arm campground is at mile 22.2; just beyond that is the Elk Wallow store and picnic area.

At Panorama, mile 31.5, is the Thornton Gap Entrance Station where the drive crosses U.S. Highway 211. U.S. highway 211 goes west to Luray, New Market, and Interstate 81; it goes east to Sperryville, Culpeper, and Warrenton and the Virginia suburbs of Washington, D.C.

Drives 1 and 4 are nearby: Drive 1 to the west traverses the Shenandoah Valley; Drive 4 to the east has excellent views of the Blue Ridge from the Piedmont. From Panorama, you can follow the Appalachian Trail uphill to the cliffs at Mary's Rock for excellent views of Thornton Gap.

Just beyond Panorama, the drive passes through 600-foot-long Mary's Rock Tunnel, the only tunnel on Skyline Drive. The tunnel, cut through billion-year-old metamorphic rocks, was not necessary from an engineering standpoint, but was constructed to provide variety along the drive.

Luray and the Shenandoah Valley spread out in the distance.

Stony Man Mountain, with its step-like profile, looms straight ahead at the overlook at mile 38.6. The steeper cliffs are formed in resistant basalt rocks of the Catoctin lava flows. The peak is 4,010 feet high, second highest in the park. To the right in the Shenandoah Valley lies the town of Luray. The gap on the horizon is New Market Pass in Massanutten Mountain.

A half-mile beyond is the trailhead for the Little Stony Man Cliffs, which follows along the base of one of the lava flows. Longer, circular hikes can also start here.

The Hemlock Springs Overlook at mile 39.1 formerly revealed many dead and near-dead hemlocks. Hemlock leaves are a favorite food of the gypsy moth caterpillar. Many of the dead trees were knocked down by a severe ice storm in 1988, and have since been removed, improving the view. Over the years the scenery at many overlooks has slowly became obstructed by the growth of underbrush, shrubs, and small trees; in recent years the National Park Service has been cutting back the shrubbery and restoring the view.

The turnoff for Skyland at mile 41.7 is the highest point on the drive, at 3,680 feet. Just inside the turnoff is the trailhead for the Stony Man Nature Trail. This 1.5-mile, round-trip hike probably gives you the best view for the effort of any hike in the park. A brochure guides you along 20 interpretive signs, culminating at the rocky summit of Stony Man Mountain, which you saw earlier from the road. Nearby are several nesting sites for the endangered peregrine falcon—known for its high-speed dives—which the National Park Service has been successfully reintroducing.

Skyland itself, with its lodge, dining room, gift shop, stables, and riding horses, is a popular destination for some travelers. Rangers conduct guided walks and evening programs. The resort was established in the 1890s by naturalist George Pollock, whose continuing efforts helped to establish the park.

Back on the drive, at mile 42.6, is the trailhead for White Oak Canyon, known for its waterfalls. The first waterfall requires a 4.6-mile down-and-up hike; to visit all six is even more strenuous.

The least strenuous hike in the park is just past White Oak Canyon: the wheelchair-accessible Limberlost Trail. The trail passes through groves of red spruce and hemlocks, some of the largest and oldest trees in the park. Hemlocks, some more than 400 years old, have become endangered through the action of an exotic insect, the hemlock woolly adelgid. These tiny bugs feed on nutrients in the hemlock needles, eventually weakening and killing the tree.

The best view of Hawksbill Mountain, at 4,051 feet the highest in the park, is from the Crescent Rock Overlook at mile 44.4. Trailheads at miles 45.6 and 46.7 lead to the summit and an unsurpassed 360-degree view of mountains in all directions.

The waterfall closest to Skyline Drive is the 70-foot cascades of Dark Hollow Falls. It is about a 1.5-mile round trip from the trailhead at mile 50.7.

Just beyond the Dark Hollow trailhead is Big Meadows, the largest open treeless area in the park. In the 1920s much of the future park had been cut for timber and looked like this. This flat plain is known for its wildflowers, strawberries, and blueberries, which attract grouse, mice, rabbits, deer, and other birds and animals.

Turn into the Big Meadows facilities at either mile 51.0 or 51.9. The Byrd Visitor Center, named for former Virginia Senator Harry F. Byrd, contains numerous exhibits and information on activities, including guided nature hikes along several nearby trails.

A trail of historical interest takes you to Camp Hoover where President Herbert Hoover came to relax and to escape the pressures of Washington. Several original structures can be seen at the site, including the President's cabin. Other facilities at Big Meadows are a restaurant and store, gas station, the Big Meadows Lodge, and a campground.

Children may enjoy the self-guided Story of the Forest Nature Trail accessible by paved trail from the Byrd Center or at mile 51.2. This 2-mile round-trip walk has 22 interpretive signs describing forest sights and ecology.

The Bearfence Mountain trail at mile 56.4 is a strenuous, 0.8-mile round-trip scramble, much of it over jumbled rocks to an excellent 360-degree view. Along the way you'll pass numerous trees downed by Hurricane Fran in 1996, and huge boulders of Catoctin greenstone.

It's a "Four Ridge Day" on Skyline Drive. On exceptionally clear days, five or even six parallel ridges are visible.

A picnic area and another campground are at Lewis Mountain at mile 57.5. A few aging cabins are available for overnight stays.

At the South River picnic area, mile 62.8, is the trailhead to South River Falls. This is a strenuous, 4.5-mile, round-trip hike to an 83-foot-high waterfall.

The drive crosses U.S. Highway 33 and the Swift Run Entrance Station at mile 65.7. To the west, US 33 goes to the West Virginia border; to the east it goes to Stanardsville and U.S. Highway 29.

The Loft Mountain Information Center at mile 79.5 has a campground, gasoline, and a gift shop. The Loft Mountain trail is a moderate, 2.7-mile loop with views of Flat Top Mountain and to the east, the Piedmont.

The valley at Big Run, to the left of the overlook at mile 81.5, is almost entirely enclosed by mountains. Heavy rains from the large watershed occasionally fill the narrow outlet with resultant floods. At mile 83.7 is the entrance to the Dundo Group Camp, a former Civilian Conservation Corps (CCC) center. The campground is open only to organized groups on a reservation basis.

Numerous dead trees, victims of the gypsy moth caterpillar, line both sides of the drive for the next several miles. Although new growth will eventually replace the old forest, the dead trees will be around for years, perhaps creating a fire hazard as they fall and line the forest floor.

Calf Mountain at mile 98.9 provides a 360-degree view. You can see the full width of the Shenandoah Valley, undivided here by Massanutten Mountain. The drive and park narrow beyond here to little more than a road bordered by a fence.

The road descends to the entrance station and then to Rockfish Gap to end at mile 105.4 at Interstate 64 and U.S. Highway 250. Go east (left) to go to Charlottesville, or go west (right) to Waynesboro and I-81. The Blue Ridge Parkway (Drives 6 and 7) begins just across I-64; the Humpback Visitor Center is 5 miles south.

6

Blue Ridge Parkway North
Rockfish Gap to Roanoke

General description: The northern section of the Blue Ridge Parkway in Virginia is a paved, two-lane, mountain drive along the ridgetops of the Southern Appalachians from near Charlottesville to Roanoke. The 121-mile drive winds up and down along the mountain crests from a low elevation of about 650 feet to almost 4,000 feet, with numerous scenic viewpoints and overlooks. This section is surrounded by the trees, shrubs, and flowers of George Washington and Jefferson National Forests.

Special attractions: The forest and scenic mountain views are rightfully the main attractions of the drive. Some special areas to visit are the Otter Creek Recreation Area along the James River, and the Peaks of Otter in the shadow of Sharp Top Mountain. Near Roanoke is Virginia's Explore Park, and the 4-mile Roanoke Mountain Loop Drive.

Location: West-central Virginia.

Drive route numbers: Blue Ridge Parkway. There are no route numbers.

Travel season: Travel is heaviest on weekends during the summer months, and on weekends in late September and early October when autumn leaf colors are at their most brilliant. The parkway is open all year, but portions may be closed temporarily during winter storms. Campgrounds are open during the warmer months. The only year-round lodging and facilities are at the Peaks of Otter, mile 86.0.

Camping: Campgrounds on this section of the parkway are at Otter Creek, Peaks of Otter, and Roanoke Mountain. The U.S. Forest Service maintains a campground at Sherando Lake in George Washington National Forest, near mile 16.

Services: Gasoline, restaurants, motels, and hotels are available in Roanoke and Waynesboro. The larger towns near the parkway, including Buena Vista, Lexington, Lynchburg, and Bedford, also have complete services. Gasoline is also available at Rockfish Gap. Along the parkway gasoline, a restaurant, and year-round lodging are available at Peaks of Otter, mile 86. Restaurants are also found at Whetstone Ridge, mile 29, and Otter Creek, mile 60.9.

Nearby attractions: The P. Buckley Moss Museum in Waynesboro has numerous works of its namesake artist, known for her paintings of Shenandoah Valley scenery and people. Drive 5 (Skyline Drive through Shenandoah National Park) terminates at the northern end of this drive, and Drive 7 (Blue Ridge Parkway South) is a continuation of the drive.

Drive 6: Blue Ridge Parkway North
Rockfish Gap to Roanoke

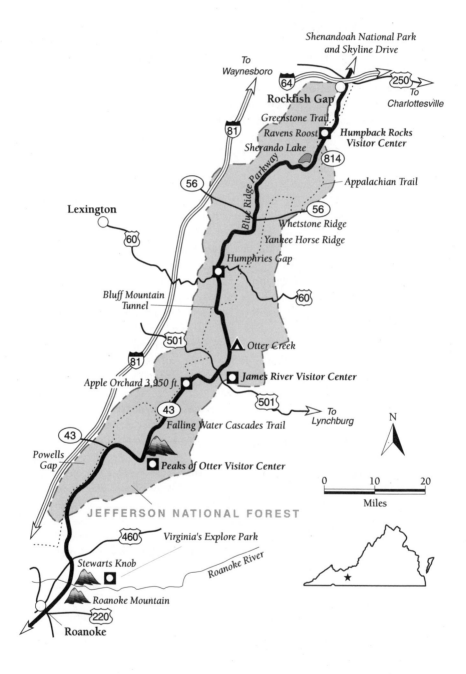

Shenandoah National Park
and Skyline Drive

To
Waynesboro

64

250

To
Charlottesville

Rockfish Gap

Greenstone Trail

81

Ravens Roost

**Humpback Rocks
Visitor Center**

Sherando Lake

814

56

Blue Ridge Parkway

Appalachian Trail

Lexington

56

Whetstone Ridge

Yankee Horse Ridge

60

Humphries Gap

Bluff Mountain
Tunnel

60

501

Otter Creek

81

James River Visitor Center

Apple Orchard 3,950 ft.

501

To
Lynchburg

43

Falling Water Cascades Trail

N

43

Powells
Gap

Peaks of Otter Visitor Center

0   10   20

Miles

JEFFERSON NATIONAL FOREST

460

Virginia's Explore Park

Roanoke River

Stewarts Knob

Roanoke Mountain

220

Roanoke

Because the parkway extends along much of the most scenic mountain country of western Virginia, there are numerous attractions along the way, including George Washington and Jefferson National Forests, Charlottesville, Lexington (Drive 12), Natural Bridge, Buchanan (Drive 17), Smith Mountain Lake, Booker T. Washington National Monument, and the many attractions around Roanoke.

 # The Drive

The Blue Ridge Parkway is a ridgetop road that stretches 469 miles along the crest of the Appalachian Mountains linking Shenandoah National Park in Virginia and Great Smoky Mountains National Park in Tennessee and North Carolina. This drive covers the northern half of the Virginia section of the parkway, a 121-mile, up-and-down drive from Rockfish Gap to Roanoke. The southern half of the parkway, from Roanoke to the North Carolina border, is described in Drive 7.

A parkway connecting the two national parks was the suggestion of then-Senator Harry F. Byrd to President Franklin D. Roosevelt in the early 1930s. Although construction started in 1935 by Civilian Conservation Corps workers, it took five decades until the last 7-mile section, around Grandfather Mountain in North Carolina, was complete. The popularity of the drive probably far exceeds anything Senator Byrd envisioned: Today more than 17 million people visit some portion of the parkway each year.

The parkway was designed to harmonize with the natural beauty of the mountains and to preserve the historical and cultural features of the area, long a home to mountain farmers and hunters.

The winding, two-lane paved road has a speed limit of 45 miles per hour, but you'll often want to go slower to enjoy the scenery. The drive skirts along the ridgeline, with occasional dips through gaps (passes). There are several visitor centers, campgrounds, restaurants, lodging facilities, and more than 200 scenic turnouts scattered along the drive.

The Blue Ridge Parkway is maintained by the National Park Service. All plants and animals are protected. There is no fee, and you can enter and leave the parkway at numerous intersections. The mileage is posted on cement markers every mile, beginning at Rockfish Gap, mile zero. Mileages are shown here to the nearest tenth.

The Virginia portion of the parkway is about 217 miles long. This drive covers the northern 121 miles of the parkway, from Rockfish Gap to U.S. Highway 220 outside Roanoke. Except for the few miles before Roanoke, this section is surrounded by heavily wooded George Washington and Jefferson National Forests with few intersections.

The parkway and the drive begin at Rockfish Gap. The entrance is at the intersection of Exit 99 of Interstate 64 and U.S. Highway 250, about 3 miles east of Waynesboro and 20 miles west of Charlottesville. It is directly across the highway from the southern terminus of Skyline Drive in Shenandoah National Park (Drive 5). Mileage markers are posted every mile. The Appalachian Trail, the ridgetop hiking trail from Maine to Georgia, parallels the parkway with numerous access points from Rockfish Gap to mile 103.

Head south on the parkway on the steeply climbing road. Views of the Shenandoah Valley to the right and the Piedmont to the left slowly unfold as you ascend to the crest of the Blue Ridge. The Humpback Rocks area, from about mile 5 to mile 10, has a self-guiding trail past several reconstructed pioneer log buildings, and several other short trails. The Greenstone Trail (mile 8.8) leads 0.2 mile through an oak and hickory forest to outcrops of the Catoctin greenstone, an extensive late Precambrian lava flow exposed in many of the road cuts. Ask here or at any of the visitor centers for maps and information on this and other hiking trails.

At Ravens Roost, mile 10.7, are broad views of Torry Mountain and the Shenandoah Valley. For the next several miles, snapped and broken tops of many of the trees attest to the extensive ice storm damage that occurred the winter of 1997–1998.

Sherando Lake, a recreation area in George Washington National Forest, is accessible at mile 16 via Virginia Highway 814. The lake, 4.5 miles from the parkway, features swimming, picnicking, and camping.

The drive continues along the ridgeline, with numerous turnoffs and views. At mile 17.6 is a view of the Priest, tallest of the "Religious Mountains," that also include the Cardinal, Friar, Little Priest, and—no trees on the summit—Bald Friar.

Whetstone Ridge, where mountaineers sharpened their knives and axes, has gasoline and a small store at mile 29. The "whetstone" is a fine-grained sandstone deposited as invading seas covered the greenstone lava in early Cambrian time about 560 million years ago..

Until the early 1900s, lumbering was second only to farming as the region's most important industry, and many of the mountain slopes were clear-cut. The most prized wood was that of the horse chestnut; unfortunately, the chestnut trees that were not cut down were all killed by the chestnut blight in the 1930s. The logs were hauled out by mule and horse. At Yankee Horse Ridge, mile 34.4, is a reconstructed spur of an old logging railroad that ran along the ridge. A ten-minute trail leads to a logging exhibit and small waterfall.

The drive descends to Humphries Gap, mile 45.6, and crosses U.S. Highway 60. Lexington, the starting point for Drive 12, is about 11 miles to the west.

Turn on your lights as you drive through the 630-foot-long Bluff Mountain Tunnel, just past mile 53 and the only Virginia tunnel on the parkway.

Soon you reach Otter Creek, which the drive follows downhill several miles to the James River. This recreation area is popular with hikers, anglers, and picnickers. The campground at the Otter Creek Recreation Area, mile 60.8, is scattered along the hemlocks, oaks, pines, and mountain laurel. The recreation area is also equipped with a visitor center, restaurant, and gift shop; there are several short trails and occasional naturalist-led walks.

Just past the recreation area, mile 61.6, Virginia Route 130 leads west 15 miles to Natural Bridge. At mile 63.8 you reach the James River overlook and visitor center and the lowest elevation on the parkway, 649 feet above sea level.

Until the advent of the railroad in the late 1800s, the James River was an important transportation link through the mountains. A footbridge spans the river, a favorite spot for anglers, with views both upstream and down through the river gorges. Across the river you can examine several restored locks of the James River and Kanawha Company; its builders planned to cross the mountains by canal and reach the Ohio River. But railroads replaced the canals and towpaths, and the project was abandoned.

Back on the drive you cross the James River and U.S. Highway 501. Although it is not marked, the drive here leaves the George Washington National Forest and enters the Jefferson National Forest. In a few miles the drive climbs out of the river valley. At mile 72.6 is a good view back to the James River.

The drive reaches its highest elevation in Virginia, 3,950 feet, at the Apple Orchard turnout, mile 76.5. (The highest point on the parkway, 6,047 feet, is at mile 431 in North Carolina.)

The parking area at mile 83.1 is the trailhead for the Falling Water Cascades Trail, a segment of the National Recreation Trail. This is a moderate loop hike of 1.6 miles through thick stands of rhododendron to a lacy cascade fringed by hemlocks. It involves a change in elevation, both up and down, of about 260 feet.

Just beyond, at mile 86.0, is the Peaks of Otter Recreation Area. Dominating the scene is conical 3,875-foot-high Sharp Top Mountain, and its taller but less conspicuous neighbor, 4,001-foot-high Flat Top Mountain, at one time thought to be the highest point in Virginia. The two peaks are composed of a dark granite more than a billion years old.

The Peaks of Otter has been a resort area since colonial days. In the early 1800s, Polly Woods operated her ordinary (inn) for travelers. Visitors today can dine in the restored ordinary and stay overnight in the Peaks of Otter Lodge (open all year) or camp in the campground.

Other facilities include a store, gas station, gift shop, and visitor center. Hikers have a variety of trails to choose from, including the strenuous

Mules once pulled barges through this restored lock of the James River and Kanawha Company, but the faster and cheaper railroads forced the company out of business.

Sharp Top Trail. The 360-degree view from the top takes in the Piedmont, Blue Ridge Mountains, Shenandoah Valley, and the distant Allegheny Mountains. If you don't want to walk, a concession-operated bus can whisk you to the top. There are frequent naturalist-conducted hikes and evening programs.

The drive continues around the big curve through Powell's Gap. Six species of oak are common to the forest, and at mile 90.0 you can examine all six of them: red, black, white, scarlet, chestnut, and bear. If leaves are on the trees, an exhibit will help you find and identify them all.

A mile past there, Virginia Route 43 leads right 5 miles to Interstate 81 and Buchanan, the start of Drive 17.

As you continue south, the ridgeline starts to narrow and you begin the long descent to the valley floor. At mile 99.6 is a view of the Roanoke Valley and the Great Valley beyond, the continuation south of the Shenandoah Valley. Gradually you emerge from the forest to views of open fields.

Houses become more frequent after you cross U.S. Highway 460 at mile 105.8. The last peak of note is Stewarts Knob, almost at the bottom of the long grade, viewed from the turnout at mile 110.6. In the other direction is a panoramic view of downtown Roanoke.

The drive becomes somewhat urbanized as it skirts the southern edge of Roanoke, the largest settlement on the parkway. You pass over the Roanoke River on a high bridge; on the other side is the Roanoke River Parking Overlook. A path leads to a view 100 feet above the river gorge. The railroad along the river is the Norfolk and Western, which hauls coal from western Virginia and West Virginia. The railroad has its headquarters in downtown Roanoke.

At mile 115.8 the Roanoke River Parkway leads left in 1.5 miles to Virginia's Explore Park, a frontier museum that emphasizes the state's role in western expansion. Among its exhibits are a working blacksmith shop, a nineteenth-century school, a farm with friendly animals, and a tavern, all presented by guides in authentic period clothing. A fee is charged.

East of Roanoke is Smith Mountain Lake, a popular resort area. Near the lake is the Booker T. Washington National Monument, marking the birthplace of this leading African-American educator.

At mile 120.3 is the entrance to the 4-mile loop road over Roanoke Mountain, with good views of the city and a short trail. The loop drive is steep and winding and is not open to trailers. It is closed at dusk and during inclement weather. Just past the loop drive is the entrance to the Roanoke Mountain Campground.

The drive ends at U.S. Highway 220, at mile 121.4, about 4 miles from downtown Roanoke. But the Blue Ridge Parkway continues and the section from Roanoke to North Carolina is described in Drive 7.

Roanoke is known for its museums, including the hands-on exhibits and planetarium at the celebrated Science Museum of Western Virginia. Close to the parkway is the Mill Mountain Zoo. On top of Mill Mountain is the 100-foot-high Roanoke Star, whose beacons of light shine down nightly on the city.

A pioneer cabin typical of the 1800s has been reconstructed at Humpback Rocks.

7

Blue Ridge Parkway South
Roanoke to North Carolina

General description: This 97-mile section of the Blue Ridge Parkway is a two-lane road along the edge of the Blue Ridge plateau with alternating views of mountains, the Piedmont, forests, and nearby farms. Many restorations and exhibits of eighteenth-century mountain life add to the interest. There are several hikes to points of interest along the drive.

Special attractions: The scenic views of woods, farms, and distant vistas are outstanding. The most popular stop is the restored Mabry Mill and water wheel and other buildings. At Smart View is a restored mountain cabin and farm by a small lake. Ground Hog Mountain contains samples of types of old wooden fences.

Location: South-central Virginia beginning at Roanoke.

Drive route numbers: Blue Ridge Parkway. There is no route number.

Travel season: Travel is heaviest during the summer months and on weekends in late September and early October when autumn leaf colors are at their most brilliant. The parkway is open all year, but portions may be closed temporarily during winter storms.

Camping: Camping is available from around May 1 through the end of October at Rocky Knob. You can also camp at Fairy Stone State Park, about 24 miles from the exit at Tuggle Gap, mile 165.3.

Services: Gasoline, restaurants, motels, and hotels are abundantly available in Roanoke. Gasoline is not available along the drive. A restaurant at Mabry Mill is the only food service along this part of the parkway.

Nearby attractions: The Roanoke area has several points of interest; these are described in Drive 6. The towns of Floyd and Galax are famed for their mountain music.

 The Drive

This 97-mile drive follows the Blue Ridge Parkway south from Roanoke to the North Carolina line. The Blue Ridge Parkway is a ridgetop road that stretches 469 miles along the crest of the southern Appalachian Mountains linking Shenandoah National Park in Virginia and Great Smoky Mountains National Park in Tennessee and North Carolina. The northern section of the Virginia portion of the parkway is described in Drive 6.

Drive 7: Blue Ridge Parkway South
Roanoke to North Carolina

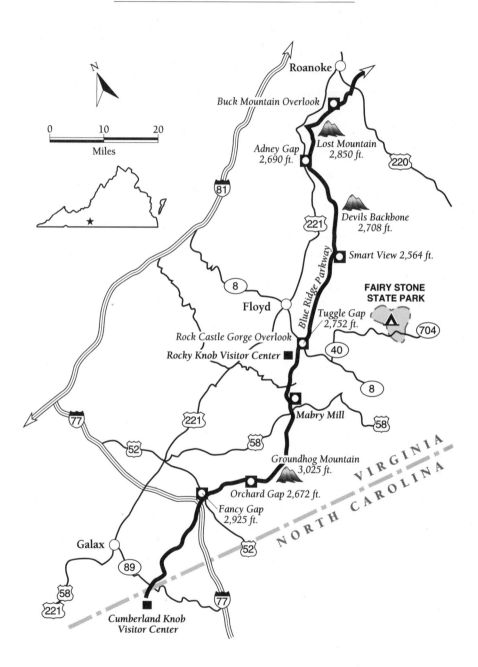

N

0   10   20
Miles

81

Roanoke

Buck Mountain Overlook

Lost Mountain 2,850 ft.

Adney Gap 2,690 ft.

220

221

Devils Backbone 2,708 ft.

Smart View 2,564 ft.

8

FAIRY STONE STATE PARK

Floyd

Tuggle Gap 2,752 ft.

704

Rock Castle Gorge Overlook

Blue Ridge Parkway

40

Rocky Knob Visitor Center

8

77

221

Mabry Mill

58

52

58

Groundhog Mountain 3,025 ft.

VIRGINIA

Orchard Gap 2,672 ft.

NORTH CAROLINA

Fancy Gap 2,925 ft.

52

Galax

89

58

221

77

Cumberland Knob Visitor Center

This section of the drive follows the high eastern rim of the Blue Ridge escarpment past farms, woods, and small towns. Much of the land bordering the parkway is leased to farmers or privately owned, with crops growing almost to the right-of-way. The farms alternate with open areas and lush forests of pines and hardwoods. Old rail fences line the road in many places, with century-old log cabins and modern farmhouses in the background. The road climbs to the top of the escarpment for distant views of the Piedmont and Appalachian Mountains and then dips through low gaps and broad valleys.

The winding, two-lane, paved road has a speed limit of 45 miles per hour with frequent scenic turnouts and major exhibits at Smart View (mile 154.5), Rocky Knob (169.0), and Mabry Mill (mile 176.1). The Blue Ridge Parkway is maintained by the National Park Service. All plants and animals are protected. There is no fee, and you can enter and leave the parkway at numerous intersections. The mileage is posted on cement markers every mile. Mileage is shown here to the nearest tenth.

The drive starts outside Roanoke at mile 121.4 at the junction of U.S. Highway 220 where Drive 6 ends. If you haven't visited the Roanoke area or taken Drive 6, you may want to refer to it for points of interest in Roanoke and north along the parkway in the Roanoke area.

Wooden fences come in many styles. This exhibit at Ground Hog Mountain shows snake fence (left) and buck fence.

Head south on the parkway, along the valley of the Roanoke River. At the Buck Mountain Overlook, mile 123.2, a 0.5-mile trail leads to the summit and a scenic, but urban, view of southern Roanoke.

Then begins the long climb up the Blue Ridge escarpment. Several turnouts provide views of the Roanoke Valley. Perhaps the best is at Lost Mountain, mile 129.9, where in one direction you can see the spine of the Blue Ridge, and in the other, the parallel ridges of the Valley and Ridge province. Nobody seems to know why this is called Lost Mountain. The mountain isn't lost, but the reason for its name is.

In the frequent open areas are fields of grazing cattle and horses. Farmers till the rolling fields planted in corn, soybean, oats, and other crops, their homes, silos, and barns nearby. Timeless dirt roads, looking much as they did 100 years ago, parallel and cross the parkway, leading you to envision couples holding hands in a horse and carriage.

In other places forests of pine, oak, hickory, and birch surround the roadway, along with thick growths of rhododendron, dogwood, and mountain laurel. The result is a feeling that the parkway belongs here, that it fits in with the scenery and history of this peaceful land.

The Smart View Recreation Area, mile 154.5, has picnic grounds by a small pond. A short trail takes you to an 1890s log cabin where you'll see "a right smart" view. The one-room cabin itself, with its rough-cut logs, garden, and nearby spring, is typical of many mountain dwellings and was lived in until the 1920s.

At Tuggle Gap, mile 165.3, Virginia Route 8 leads 4 miles north to Floyd, long famed as a mountain-music center. (Another mountain-music center is Galax, near mile 216.) The parkway actively participates in these music programs, helping to preserve this cultural and entertaining heritage.

VA 8 leads east 24 miles from Tuggle Gap to Fairy Stone State Park. The "fairy stones" are twinned crystals of the mineral staurolite, which intersect to form a cross. No fairy story, however, was a 50-pound channel catfish caught in the park's lake. The park also features a campground, swimming, and boating.

As you approach the Rocky Knob Visitor Center you'll see rocks along the road standing almost straight up around miles 167 to 169. They reminded some old-timers of the fins on the back of a fish. So these are The Fins: Actually they are erosional remnants of schist and gneiss rocks that were folded almost vertically.

At mile 168.8 is an imposing view of Rock Castle Gorge. You can hike into the gorge on a strenuous, 7-mile loop trail, or stretch your legs on several shorter walks. The Rocky Knob Recreation Area also has a campground, rental cabins, and ranger-led programs. The cabins, and much of the roads and trails, were built by youths enrolled in the Civilian Conservation Corps, a government program that provided employment during the Depression.

Mabry Mill, mile 176.1, is the best-known and probably most frequently photographed spot on the entire parkway. It was built by E.B. Mabry in 1910, and remained in operation as a grist mill, sawmill, and blacksmith shop until 1935. Mabry left the coal mines of West Virginia in 1908 to work as a blacksmith. As his fortunes increased, he built the mill where he ground meal and sawed logs for his mountain neighbors.

The water wheel still turns and the mill still grinds today. You can sample the output with purchases of mill-ground cornmeal and buckwheat. Other exhibits show pioneer workshops of tanners, blacksmiths, shoemakers, and others. During summer and fall, frequent demonstrations by craftspeople bring to life the old-time skills. A gift shop and restaurant are nearby.

The drive crosses U.S. Highway 58 at mile 177.7. At Groundhog Mountain, mile 188.8, a lookout tower fashioned like a tobacco barn provides a 360-degree view. And if you've been wondering about the different types of wooden fences you've been seeing, look closely at the three kinds displayed here: snake, buck, and post and rail.

At Orchard Gap, mile 193.7, several trees from an old apple orchard are still standing. Others have been replaced by a cluster of houses.

Many old graveyards, big and small, are scattered through the woods and hills. Some are forgotten, while others are tended with care and reverence by present-day descendants. Most are hidden from the drive, tucked away in hollows. The headstone was usually a simple rock slab with a knife-scratched inscription, but some were elaborately sculpted memorials. A graveyard of the simple kind can be seen at mile 196.8.

Interstate 77 crosses the parkway at mile 200.8, but there is no access.

The last exit in Virginia is Virginia Highway 89 at mile 215. The town of Galax lies 7 miles north on VA 89. Galax is another famed center for mountain music. You can hear those fiddles playing almost any weekend, but the music builds to a crescendo the second weekend each August when the town overflows with both people and music for the Old Fiddlers' Convention. This has been an annual event since 1935.

You leave Virginia and enter North Carolina at mile 216.9. The boundary was first surveyed in 1749 by a party that included mapmaker Peter Jefferson, Thomas Jefferson's father.

The Cumberland Knob Visitor Center, with trails to Cumberland Knob, is just a little bit farther down the road, at mile 217.9. The visitor center and 12 miles of drive south of here opened in 1936; it was the first section of the parkway to be completed.

From here, you can reverse direction and go north into Virginia, or continue on the Blue Ridge Parkway into North Carolina. A detailed description of this portion of the parkway, plus other superb drives in North Carolina, is outlined in Laurence Parent's *Scenic Driving North Carolina*, also from Falcon Publishing.

8

Fredericksburg and Spotsylvania Battlefields

A Civil War Tour

General description: This is a 40-mile, historical drive through four major battlefields of the Civil War preserved in the Fredericksburg and Spotsylvania National Military Park. The drive covers the Fredericksburg Battlefield on the outskirts of Fredericksburg, and the Chancellorsville, Wilderness, and Spotsylvania Court House battlefields west of Fredericksburg. The region is one of flat or gently rolling land with a mixture of open fields and hardwood, second-growth forests.

Special attractions: The Civil War battlefields themselves are the main points of interest, with their maps, exhibits, explanations, and tours.

Location: The battlefields and drive are located both in Fredericksburg and west of town within a 15-mile radius. Fredericksburg is in eastern Virginia about 50 miles south of Washington, D.C., and 60 miles north of Richmond on Interstate 95.

Drive route numbers: U.S. Highway Business 1; Virginia Highways 638, 636, 208, 613, 621, 3, 610, and 20; and several local roads within the battlefields.

Travel season: All year.

Services: Motels, restaurants, and gasoline are available in Fredericksburg and along Virginia Highway 3 west of Fredericksburg.

Nearby attractions: Fredericksburg, George Washington's hometown for many years, has numerous restored colonial buildings.

 The Drive

This 40-mile loop tours the four battlefields—Fredericksburg, Chancellorsville, Wilderness, and Spotsylvania Court House—preserved in Fredericksburg and Spotsylvania National Military Park in Fredericksburg and vicinity. The drive begins and ends in Fredericksburg and extends west of the city about 15 miles. The country outside the city is gently rolling with a mixture of open fields and farms, hardwood forests, rural houses, and some suburban housing. The park areas have been partially restored to look as they did at the time of the Civil War.

To make the drive as scenic as possible, the battlefields are not visited in chronological order, and the drive varies from the self-guiding tours set up by the National Park Service, which pass through several shopping mall areas. If you are a Civil War buff whose main interest is history and battle strategy, you probably will prefer to follow the detailed, more direct, but less scenic, route laid out by the Park Service.

Fredericksburg, home of Mary Washington College, has many restored colonial homes, including 300 original buildings built before 1870. More than 100 of these pre-date the extensive destruction wrought on the town during the Civil War. Fredericksburg was also the hometown of the Washington family, including George, his mother, sister, and brother; some of the restored buildings were Washington-family residences. Fredericksburg is also the starting point for Drive 9, the Northern Neck, and is described in more detail in that drive.

The drive begins at the Fredericksburg Battlefield Visitor Center on the outskirts of Fredericksburg. At the start of the Civil War the town was a bustling river port on the Rappahannock River with a population of about 5,000. Its prime location, halfway between the Federal capital at Washington, D.C., and the Confederate capital at Richmond, made it a strategic Civil War target for both sides. Over a two-year period more than 600,000 men fought here in four major battles; more than 100,000 died.

The visitor center features audio-visual programs, exhibits, detailed maps, battle tour information, and publications. A fee is charged. Outside the visitor center you can walk up the short hill to Mary's Heights, now a national cemetery for 15,000 Civil War soldiers.

In the First Battle of Fredericksburg, December 11–13, 1862, Confederate General Robert E. Lee successfully fought off the invading Federal troops. This battle gave Lee his most one-sided victory of the war, but the price was high: 12,000 Federal and 5,000 Confederate troops died in this conflict, prompting Lee after his bittersweet victory to make his famous remark, "It is well that war is so terrible—else we should grow too fond of it."

To begin the actual drive, turn right on Business Route US 1 as you leave the visitor center. Go about a half-mile and turn left on Lee Drive to enter the battlefield. For 4 miles the drive follows part of the almost continuous, 7-mile, sinuous line of Confederate trenches dug for the 1862 battle. Although the area surrounding the park is now urbanized, the drive passes through hardwood groves with abundant rhododendron bushes. Exhibits at several turnoffs help interpret the battle.

At the stop sign cross VA 638 and continue on Lee Drive. It dead-ends at a parking area at Prospect Hill, where the Federal troops broke through the Confederate line. You can also see the 20-foot-high Southern Memorial Pyramid built after the war to be visible from the adjacent railroad.

Turn around and retrace your steps about 2 miles to the stop sign. Turn left on VA 638, go less than a mile, and turn right on VA 636. Virginia Highway 636 meanders through suburbia, crossing US 1, to a traffic light at

Drive 8: Fredericksburg and Spotsylvania Battlefields

A Civil War Tour

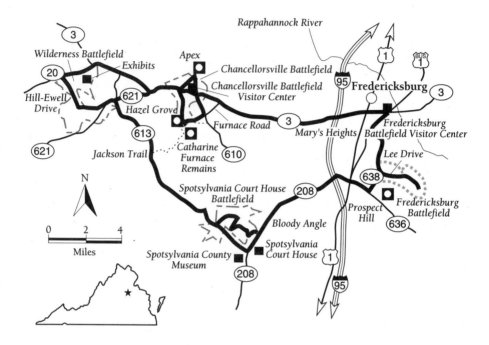

VA 208, also known as Court House Road. Turn left on four-lane VA 208 toward Spotsylvania Court House.

The houses soon thin out, replaced by woods, cattle farms, and barns as you drive over gently rolling ground. About 4 miles from the traffic light, just before the road becomes two lanes, you pass a narrow road on the right. This is the exit for the one-way loop through Spotsylvania Court House Battlefield; you will pass this spot again after touring the battlefield.

On the left, just before the town of Spotsylvania Court House (sometimes known simply as Spotsylvania), is a Confederate cemetery containing the remains of about 570 Confederate soldiers killed in the fighting around Spotsylvania.

VA 208 ends in town at a T-intersection with VA 613. Just to the left of this intersection is the Spotsylvania County Museum. Originally the Old Berea Church, the small brick building, which was heavily damaged during the fighting in 1864, contains relics from the battlefield and several dioramas.

When you leave the museum, turn left on VA 613 and continue past the intersection with VA 208. In a few moments you pass the Robert E. Lee

Elementary School; the name may or may not reflect the political leanings of the area.

Turn right in about a mile at the entrance to the Spotsylvania Court House Battlefield and go to the exhibit shelter on the left. The Battle of Spotsylvania took place in May 1864, after the stalemate at the Wilderness Battlefield a few days earlier. (You will pass through the Wilderness Battlefield later on this drive.) Spotsylvania Court House was a 14-day fight ending in defeat for Lee and the Confederate troops. It was a major step in Grant's drive south leading to Lee's surrender at Appomattox less than a year later. (Drive 13, Lee's Retreat, covers this final campaign of the Civil War.) Maps and displays help explain the complex military maneuvers during the two-week battle. The exhibit shelter is also the starting point for a 7-mile walking tour of the battlefield.

From the exhibits continue for about a mile to the parking area at the Bloody Angle, scene of some of the most ferocious fighting of the entire war. During a 23-hour battle May 12–13, 1864, Grant's troops captured 20 cannons and most of a Confederate division. In brutal, face-to-face engagement, men fired at point-blank range and slaughtered each other with bayonets and clubs. During the intense fighting, an oak tree 22 inches in diameter was cut down by the deadly hail of small-arms fire.

The Bloody Angle today consists of rolling, pastoral fields and quiet woods. A few Confederate trenches and interpretive signs are the only reminders of its savage history where more than 20,000 soldiers died. From the parking lot you can cover the entire battlefield in a 30-minute walking tour; folders are available at the site.

The drive through the battle area winds past woods and open fields. Spurs lead to the trenches at Lee's Final Line and the site of several houses used as headquarters during the battle. The road curves and leads to East Angle for another view of the Bloody Angle.

Sporadic fighting continued at Spotsylvania until May 21, 1864, when Grant pulled his troops out and began his drive south, toward Richmond, Petersburg, and the end of the war, at Appomattox.

Past East Angle the road becomes one-way. Follow it under overhanging trees to the stop sign at VA 208. Turn right on VA 208. This is the part of the drive that is repeated. Follow VA 208 to the T-intersection at VA 613 in the town of Spotsylvania Court House. Turn right. Continue straight on VA 613 this time, past the entrance to Spotsylvania Court House Battlefield.

Follow winding VA 613 through wooded glens for about 7 miles and turn right at the intersection with VA 621, known in Civil War days as the Orange Plank Road. VA 621 ends in about 2 miles at four-lane VA 3. Turn right on VA 3 one mile and turn left into the visitor center at the entrance to Chancellorsville Battlefield.

This chimney is all that remains of Catharine Furnace, a Confederate munitions plant, which was destroyed by Union troops in 1864 during the Battle of the Wilderness.

Maps and detailed battle descriptions are available at the visitor center. The Battle of Chancellorsville in May 1863 was the South's greatest victory, when Lee defeated Federal General Joseph Hooker by a brilliant flanking attack. During the battle Confederate General Stonewall Jackson, returning from the front, was mistakenly shot by his own troops. Jackson's arm had to be amputated, and he was so weakened by his wounds that he developed pneumonia and died a few days later.

When you leave the visitor center, follow the one-way road through stands of redbud and rhododendron to the Apex, site of Hooker's last line. Turn right on VA 610. At the stop sign at VA 3, VA 610 passes the site of the Chancellorsville Inn, a popular pub and meeting place before the Civil War, and used as headquarters by General Hooker.

Cross VA 3 and go about a mile on VA 610 to unnumbered Furnace Road. Turn right on Furnace Road, which follows the route of Jackson's Flank March. Soon you come to the Catharine Furnace Ruins, site of an early nineteenth-century iron foundry. Although closed before the Civil War, it was reopened to manufacture Confederate munitions before it was destroyed by Federal troops in 1864.

Turn right at Catharine Furnace. Bear left at the intersection, passing the cannons at the high ground at Hazel Grove. Because trees and heavy underbrush covered much of the area, artillery was infrequently used during most of the battles. But at the open ground in Hazel Grove, Confederate troops took over the area from retreating Federals and opened fire on the Northern troops.

Across the highway from the Chancellorsville Visitor Center, turn left on VA 3. Go about 2 miles and turn left on VA 20, which enters the Wilderness Battlefield. Drive about 1.3 miles to the exhibits for a detailed explanation of this encounter.

The Battle of the Wilderness, in early May 1864, was the first time Grant and Lee met in combat. It ended in an apparent stalemate. The battle gets its name from the thick underbrush and dense thickets that obscured views for both troops. In the heavy woods, confused troops could not tell friend from foe. Inexperienced and frightened soldiers fired at the slightest provocation, real or perceived, and many soldiers were killed by their own side. Muzzle flashes from the guns set the woods on fire, resulting in severe and often fatal burns on both sides. A 2-mile-loop walking trail from the shelter traverses much of the battle area, with several views of the earthworks constructed by Union soldiers.

Continue down VA 20 for a few hundred feet when you leave the shelter, and turn left on Hill-Ewell Drive. You will notice numerous Confederate trenches beside the road. Turn left at the stop sign at VA 621.

Although the Battle of the Wilderness was a draw, Grant and Lee met in battle a few days later at Spotsylvania Court House 8 miles to the south, already described in this drive. The drive continues on VA 621 to the stop sign at VA 3.

Turn right on VA 3, passing the Chancellorsville Visitor Center again and leaving the battlefield area. Follow VA 3 about 10 miles to Fredericksburg. The last few miles pass by several malls and shopping centers. Cross I-95 and proceed into Fredericksburg.

Confederate cannons at Hazel Grove look ready to fire at the attacking Union forces.

9

Northern Neck
Fredericksburg to Reedville

General description: The Northern Neck is the stretch of land extending east of Fredericksburg between the Rappahannock and Potomac rivers. From Fredericksburg this 70-mile drive follows the shoreline of the wide tidewater Potomac, past several stops of historical, scenic, and scientific interest to end at Reedville, a fishing village on the shores of Chesapeake Bay. Along the way you'll pass through gently rolling farmland and woods, with frequent views of inlets and bays. Beach walking, historic mansions, and old fishing villages may all be of interest.

Special attractions: Historic sites include the restored birthplace of George Washington, the birthplace of James Monroe, and the aristocratic mansion and birthplace of Robert E. Lee and the Lee family. At Westmoreland State Park are swimming, camping, and picnicking along the Potomac. Beach walks give striking views of the Horsehead Cliffs and the opportunity to search for fossil whale bones and sharks' teeth. At both Westmoreland and the Caledon Natural Area, you have a chance to see bald eagles. As you approach Chesapeake Bay, you can ride on a free two-car ferry and then visit the fishing villages of Kinsale and Reedville, debarkation point for several popular boating trips to Chesapeake Bay islands.

Location: East-central Virginia. The drive starts in Fredericksburg near Exit 130 of Interstate 95, about 45 miles south of Washington, D.C., and concludes in Reedville on the shores of Chesapeake Bay.

Drive route numbers: The main drive follows U.S. Highway 360, Virginia Business 3, 218, 205, 3, 202, 604, 640, 646, 644, and 657. Side trips, mostly short spurs to points of interest, follow Virginia Highways 696, 205Y, 204, 347, 214, and 203.

Travel season: All year. The hardwood forests are very colorful in autumn; spring brings flowering dogwood and other plants. Summer is the heavy travel season and crowds can be expected on weekends at some of the beaches and attractions. Snow is rare; the bare winter trees provide long views not visible when leaves are on the trees. However, some attractions have reduced hours in winter.

Camping: Westmoreland State Park has a variety of campsites, many with RV hookups. Private campgrounds are available in Fredericksburg, Colonial Beach, and Reedsville.

Services: Motels, restaurants, and gasoline are available in Fredericksburg and most towns along the route.

Nearby attractions: Belle Isle State Park in Lancaster is under development on the southern edge of the Northern Neck along the Rappahannock River; Drive 8, Fredericksburg and Spotsylvania Battlefields, is a Civil War tour.

The Drive

The Northern Neck east of Fredericksburg is a peninsula running generally northwest to southeast, bordered by the estuaries of the Potomac River to the north and the Rappahannock River to the south. From Fredericksburg, it stretches southeast some 70 miles to the shores of Chesapeake Bay. For centuries before European exploration and settlement, it was known to the Powhatan Indians who fished and farmed here.

In the early 1600s explorer John Smith sailed up both the Potomac and Rappahannock Rivers. White settlers soon followed, to the detriment of the Native Americans, many of whom quickly succumbed to European diseases and firearms. But the white settlers flourished. The flat, rich farmland, moderate climate, and access to ocean travel made the area a major stop for trading ships during colonial days, and the Northern Neck soon became one of the most prosperous regions of the new continent.

The white shells in the foreground mark the outline of George Washington's early home, now destroyed. The brick building in the background is a reconstruction.

The families who settled here produced many of the outstanding leaders of the young United States. Along the way you will visit or pass by the birthplaces of several signers of the Declaration of Independence, three United States presidents, the commander in chief of the Confederate Army, plus several lesser-known notables.

Today nature and beauty are as important to the Northern Neck as its history. The two rivers and their scenic cliffs provide water recreation of all kinds, fossil hunting, and a home for bald eagles and other birds. The land's gently rolling, sandy surface supports extensive hardwood forests and open fields alternating with small towns, many looking much as they did 200 years ago. The eastern end of the peninsula lies along Chesapeake Bay where the economy is based on nearly equal parts of commercial fishing and recreation.

Before or after this drive, you may want to see some of Fredericksburg's attractions. The town was an important port in colonial and revolutionary days and has more than 300 original buildings built before 1870; more than 100 of these pre-date the extensive destruction wrought on the town during the Civil War.

Places of interest in Fredericksburg include the Hugh Mercer Apothecary Shop, restored to its 1771 elegance, and the Rising Sun Tavern, the town's social and political gathering place, built by George Washington's younger brother, Charles. Fredericksburg was hometown in later years to the Washington family, including George, his mother, sister, and brother. Current residents like to claim that "George Washington slept in many places, but he lived here." The town is also the starting point for Drive 8, Fredericksburg and Spotsylvania Battlefields.

To begin the drive, from downtown Fredericksburg take VA Business 3 east across the Rappahannock River bridge. Turn left a few hundred yards beyond the bridge on VA 218.

As the road climbs steeply from the river bottom, you pass the entrance on the left to Chatham Manor, a unit of Fredericksburg and Spotsylvania National Military Park. The mansion, which was used as a command post and hospital during the Civil War, has a sweeping view of Fredericksburg and the Rappahannock River.

A designated Virginia Byway, two-lane VA 218 curves its way gently up and down through pines and open fields. About 12 miles from Fredericksburg, turn left on VA 696, which leads in about a mile to Fairview Beach, a small swimming and picnic area on the banks of the Potomac River. The Potomac here is a tidewater estuary with the Maryland shore visible about 2 miles away across the water.

Retrace your route back to VA 218 and turn left. Eight miles on the left is the Caledon Natural Area, a part of the Virginia State Park system and one of the best places in the state to view bald eagles. Although some eagles are

Drive 9: Northern Neck
Fredericksburg to Reedville

To Alexandria

Caledon Natural Area

MARYLAND

Chesapeake Bay

95

Chatham Manor

BUS 3

218

646

301

Mattox Creek

Colonial Beach

Fredericksburg

3

205

Fairview Beach

George Washington's Birthplace

Stratford Hall Plantation

WESTMORELAND STATE PARK

214

Montross

Nomini Creek

360

Yeocomico River

Kinsale

N

301

3

203

Potomac River

0   5   10

Miles

Heathsville

95

Reedville

360

Rappahannock River

Fleeton

To Richmond

See detailed map

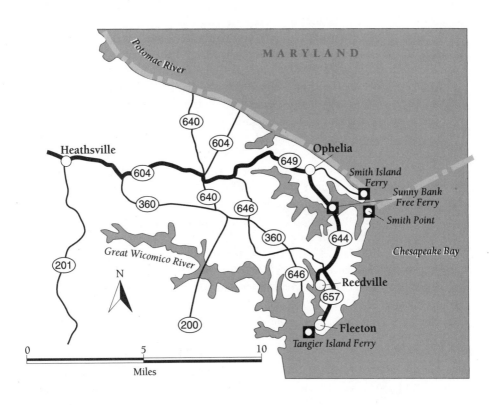

Potomac River

MARYLAND

Heathsville

640

604

604

360

201

Great Wicomico River

N

640

646

Ophelia

649

360

646

200

Smith Island
Ferry

Sunny Bank
Free Ferry

Smith Point

644

Chesapeake Bay

Reedville

657

Fleeton

Tangier Island Ferry

0   5   10
Miles

year-round residents, they are most numerous during the spring and summer nesting season along the shores of the Potomac when fish are readily available. The best way to see eagles is to join one of the mini-bus guided tours from mid-June to Labor Day. The tours also pass through some of the last stands of virgin oak-hickory forest in Virginia.

From October through March, you can hike the 3.5-mile, self-guided Boyd's Hole Trail at Caledon Natural Area, which leads to the Potomac and provides a good chance to see some of the resident eagles. All trails are subject to closure at any time to protect eagle habitat. The park also has a small visitor center and gift shop open during the warmer months, and several picnic tables adjacent to the parking area.

Continue on VA 218, bearing left where it is joined by Virginia Highway 206. Stay on VA 218 and cross four-lane U.S. Highway 301. In a few miles you cross picturesque Machodoc Creek, one of several tidewater inlets.

James Madison, fourth president of the United States, was born a few miles to the south in Port Royal in 1751; also nearby is the house where John Wilkes Booth was killed when he fled from Washington, D.C., after assassinating President Abraham Lincoln.

Virginia Highway 218 and this section of the Virginia Byway end at the junction with VA 205. Go left on VA 205. Ahead and to the left are several views of the Potomac, now several miles wide. In the resort town of Colonial Beach, turn left on VA 205Y to reach the beach, which is open to the public. If you walk along the beach and look left, you may see the US 301 bridge across the Potomac about 5 miles upstream.

Retrace VA 205Y to VA 205 and go left. Less than a mile from town you pass the birthplace of James Monroe, where there is a disappointing monument to our fifth president. The unpaved dirt turnout, marked by a simple sign and small obelisk, are a sharp contrast to the extensive and detailed memorials to George Washington and Robert E. Lee you will pass later on the drive.

There are no remnants of the Monroe family home. James Monroe was born here in 1758 and left when he was 16 to enter William and Mary College. He served in the Revolutionary War and then held a variety of government positions, including a brief term as governor of Virginia. In 1816 he was elected President of the United States, serving two terms. He is best known for the Monroe Doctrine, which declared that the Americas were no longer open to colonization by foreign countries.

The drive crosses a short causeway over Mattox Creek, another tidal inlet. A mile beyond that, VA 205 ends at the traffic light and junction with VA 3. Turn left (south) on VA 3.

The next 10 miles along VA 3 will be slow driving—not on account of traffic, but because you pass three outstanding scenic and natural attractions along this stretch: George Washington's Birthplace National Monument, Westmoreland State Park, and Robert E. Lee's birthplace at Stratford Hall.

Turn left on VA 204 to visit George Washington's Birthplace National Monument. This memorial preserves the birthplace of the first President of the United States, born here February 22, 1732, into a family of prosperous planters and farmers. Although none of the original buildings survive, modern reconstructions of a memorial house, kitchen house, dairy, and other farm buildings help to give a sense of the genteel Tidewater colonial farm life.

Slaves helped raise the main crops of tobacco, corn, and wheat. They also worked at growing other vegetables and raising farm animals for meat and hides. The location on the banks of Popes Creek, at its outlet into the Potomac River, gave access to the river highway and outside world.

As you drive onto the grounds, you are greeted by a miniature Washington Monument. The visitor center overlooks Popes Creek and is surrounded by spacious groves of mature hardwood trees. Costumed interpreters demonstrate colonial farming techniques and domestic tasks, from tobacco cultivation to soap making. The area also includes a family burial ground, picnic area, and short nature trail.

Throughout his life Washington was drawn to the Virginia side of the Potomac River, and he returned to this area whenever his busy career and obligations permitted. He lived at Popes Creek for the first two and a half years of his life, at which time his father moved the family up the Potomac to what is now known as Mount Vernon. He also lived at Popes Creek frequently during his early teen years, when the area was farmed by his half-brother, Augustine. For most of his working life Washington's home was in Fredericksburg; the city, as we have seen, claims to be Washington's hometown. His retirement years were spent at Mount Vernon (Drive 3).

Washington always considered himself to be a farmer and planter first; his other occupations—surveyor and soldier, politician and president—were but temporary interruptions in his chosen field. The site is open all year.

Return to VA 3 and turn left. In a few miles you come to VA 347 and the entrance to Westmoreland State Park. Most of the park is set on top of the 40-foot-high Horsehead Cliffs on the Potomac. Be sure to drive down the mini-canyons to reach the shore area, where you can walk along the beach and search for fossil shark teeth, whale bones, shells, and other marine animals.

The fossils are found in unconsolidated sediments of gravel, sand, silt, and clay that dip gently to the east. Similar deposits are found throughout most of the Northern Neck. The sediments here were deposited about 12 million years ago during the Miocene epoch. At that time the eastern margin of North America was still covered by the Atlantic Ocean; the ancestors of today's rivers and streams dumped large amounts of debris from the eroding

A lonely fossil hunter searches the beach by Horsehead Cliffs at Westmoreland State Park for 15-million-year-old whale bones and sharks' teeth.

Appalachian Mountains into the shallow waters. The better-known and somewhat higher Calvert Cliffs area across the Potomac in Maryland has similar deposits and fossils.

Westmoreland State Park also features swimming, picnicking, and camping in season, and several short hiking trails. The visitor center contains numerous exhibits, including representative fossils. A fee is charged during the warmer months.

Return to VA 3 and again turn left, traveling a few miles to VA 214 and the entrance to Stratford Hall Plantation, Confederate President Robert E. Lee's birthplace. Stratford Hall is far more sumptuous than Washington's birthplace. It was built in the late 1720s by Thomas Lee, a successful planter. It was also home to Thomas Lee's eight children. Two sons, Richard Henry Lee and Francis Lightfoot Lee, were the only brothers to sign the Declaration of Independence.

Their cousin, "Light Horse Harry" Lee, who also lived at Stratford Hall, was a friend of George Washington, a Revolutionary War hero, governor of Virginia, and father of Robert Edward Lee, who later became the leading general of the Confederate Army.

The brick manor, with its twin, imposing clusters of chimneys, has been carefully restored and maintained. The Great Hall in the center of the house has been designated one of the most beautiful rooms in America. Visitors can also see Robert E. Lee's cradle.

A non-profit organization maintains the plantation, including a working farm and farm animals, outbuildings, and operating grist mill. Several short hiking trails allow you to visit the shoreline and walk through the woods. Admission is charged.

Once more, return to VA 3 and turn left. At Court House Square in Montross, is the old courthouse, originally built in 1707 and now used for special events. Across the street from the courthouse is the Westmoreland County Museum, which houses a life-size portrait of William Pitt and other historical exhibits.

Just past Montross at the intersection of VA 3 and VA 202, go left on VA 202. You soon cross Nomini Creek, one of the many small tidewater rivers here. The country here is flatter and more open, with less woods and more farmland. Numerous small creeks have cut channels into the unconsolidated sediments, causing many 10- to 15-foot dips in the road.

Turn left on VA 203 for a short jaunt to Kinsale on the Yeocomico River. In the early 1700s this port was one of the busiest in Virginia, shipping almost one-third of the entire colony's products. The drive winds down Steamboat Hill to the still-active wharf. A small, free museum, open during the warmer months, describes the port's early days, and its later rise to prominence as a steamboat terminal for voyages to Baltimore and Washington.

Return to VA 202 and turn left. At the intersection with US 360, turn left. U.S. Highway 360 is primarily a three-lane highway, with occasional four-lane stretches. The town of Heathsville has several restored old buildings including Hughlett's Tavern and Rice's Inn, built in 1795, and a jail (1844) and courthouse (1851).

Continue left at the intersection on US 360 as you leave Heathsville. Two miles past Heathsville turn left on VA 604. This is an easy turn to miss. Follow this narrow, curvy road a few miles to the intersection with VA 640 and turn right. Go about a half mile and turn left on VA 646, Folly Road.

At the T-intersection in Ophelia turn right on VA 644. You will see signs for the Sunnybank Ferry, one of the state's last free ferries. The ferry, which holds two cars, carries you across the Little Wicomico River and then to Fleeton. Maintained by the Virginia Department of Transportation (VDOT), it runs year-round from 7 A.M. to 7 P.M. during daylight hours only. It does not operate on Sundays or during unusually high water. (If the ferry is not running, turn around. Follow VA 644 back to Ophelia; turn left on VA 604; turn left again on US 360 and follow it to its end in Reedville.)

After the ferry ride, continue on VA 644. At the stop sign on the outskirts of Reedville, turn left on Virginia 657. To the right, across the waters of Cockrell Creek, you will see the town of Reedville. Follow VA 657 a few miles to Fleeton. As you approach town, a sign proclaims that 89 inhabitants and

17 dogs welcome you; the numbers are crossed out and changed whenever there is an addition or subtraction.

The harbor at Fleeton has views of a lighthouse and Chesapeake Bay. Most of the town is laid out in a square with one side facing the bay. Drive around the block to reverse direction, and follow VA 657 back to the intersection with VA 644. Follow VA 644 to US 360 and turn left in Reedville, on the opposite shore of Cockrell Creek, to the end of the drive.

Reedville was established after the Civil War as a fishing port for menhaden, a small fish now used as a source of fish oil. The fish brought prosperous times to the town and one of the highest per capita incomes in the country in the late 1800s. Wealthy ship captains built rows of Victorian mansions that today line portions of Main Street. Many of these residences still have widows' walks, small, open porches on the roof where anxious wives scanned the sea hoping to spot their husband's ship returning to port.

In town is the Reedville Fisherman's Museum, open during the warmer months. It tells the story of the menhaden, which are still caught and processed here. Nearby are the terminals for the popular tour boats to Tangier Island, an old fishing village in the middle of Chesapeake Bay, and to Smith Island in Maryland.

The quiet town of Kinsale was once a busy shipping center and transportation hub for steamboat voyages to Baltimore and Washington.

10

Eastern Shore
Chincoteague to Kiptopoke

General description: The Eastern Shore of Virginia is the sandy peninsula between Chesapeake Bay and the Atlantic Ocean. It is a unique blend of land, marsh, and water, known for beaches, historic villages, NASA rockets, seafood, and unique bird and animal life. This 90-mile drive covers the peninsula from the Maryland border on the north to the southern tip, meandering back and forth from the Atlantic side to the Chesapeake Bay side.

Special attractions: Chincoteague National Wildlife Refuge and Assateague Island National Seashore, make up one of the few unspoiled stretches along the Atlantic shore, and are known for birds, beaches, marshlands, ponies, deer, and other features. These provide an interesting contrast with the space and rocket exhibits of NASA. There are numerous little historic towns, sandy beaches, and inlets, with numerous opportunities for boat trips and bird watching along both Chesapeake Bay and the Atlantic Ocean.

Location: Virginia portion of the peninsula bordered by Chesapeake Bay and the Atlantic Ocean in the extreme northeast part of the state.

Drive route numbers: U.S. Highway 13 and Business 13. Virginia Highways 175, 798, 679, 179, 178, 180, 605, 182, 639, 184, and 600. Many of these roads also have local names.

Travel season: The drive can be made all year long. Bird watching is excellent all year, but it can be particularly interesting during the spring and autumn migrations when large flocks and occasional rare species are seen. Brilliant autumn leaf colors—mostly maple, oak, and poplar—occur most years. The famous pony roundup the last week of July at Chincoteague attracts enormous crowds; summer crowds at Chincoteague are huge.

Camping: Camping is available at Assateague Island National Seashore near the northern end of the drive, and at Kiptopoke State Park near the southern end.

Services: Gasoline, restaurants, and motels are available along US 13 and in the larger towns.

Nearby attractions: Just north of the drive is the Maryland portion of Assateague Island National Seashore and Maryland's Assateague State Park and resort beaches. Connecting at the south end of the drive are the Chesapeake Bay Bridge-Tunnel, Drive 11, and the Norfolk and Virginia Beach areas.

Drive 10: Eastern Shore
Chincoteague to Kiptopoke

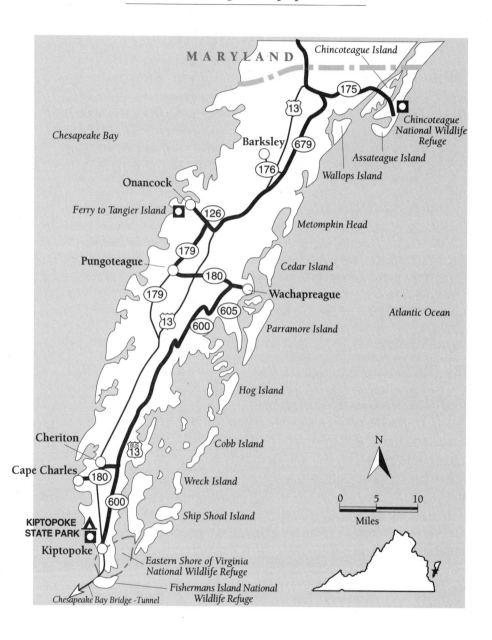

# The Drive

The Delmarva Peninsula, comprised of portions of Delaware, Maryland, and Virginia, lies between Chesapeake Bay to the west and the Atlantic Ocean to the east. The word "Delmarva" is an abbreviation for the three state names: Del-Mar-Va. The Virginia and Maryland portions are known as the Eastern Shore. From the Maryland border, the Virginia part of the Eastern Shore stretches 70 miles south to the mouth of Chesapeake Bay and the Chesapeake Bay Bridge-Tunnel (Drive 11).

No part of the Eastern Shore is more than 10 miles from water. The side facing the Atlantic is known as the Seaside; the Chesapeake side is the Bayside.

The land of the Eastern Shore consists of beach deposits and similar offshore loose sediments—mostly sand and mud—left when sea levels were higher than they are today. During the last million years, sea levels fluctuated considerably so that the Eastern Shore was alternately dry land and then covered by shallow seas. During one glacial epoch, so much water was tied up in glacial ice that sea level was about 450 feet below the present level and the Atlantic shore line was 60 miles to the east. At that time the major rivers that now form Chesapeake Bay—the Potomac and the Susquehanna—flowed in deep channels to the ocean.

When the last continental glaciers melted some 12,000 years ago, sea levels rose to about the present level, flooding the river valleys and forming Chesapeake Bay as we know it today. The river valleys of what are now the lower James, York, Rappahannock, Potomac, and other rivers that flow into Chesapeake Bay were also flooded, making Chesapeake Bay into the world's largest estuary.

Chesapeake Bay, like all estuaries, is a body of water that is fresh at one end and salty at the other, with varying degrees of brackish water in between. The water gently sloshes back and forth as the tide and rivers flowing into it change, with corresponding changes in salinity. The shallow waters of the Chesapeake Bay estuary, with its varied habitats, support many forms of life. The natural balance of nutrients flowing into the Bay is severely threatened by the large amounts of organic nitrates and industrial pollutants from various sources.

The mild climate, abundant fish and other seafood, and level, sandy farmland attracted Native Americans long before the first European settlers arrived in the early 1600s. Many towns retain their original Native American names. Despite the long history of human habitation, the Eastern Shore is known today for its miles of unspoiled beaches, marshlands, and wildlife preserves—the better known of which are Chincoteague National Wildlife

Refuge and Assateague Island National Seashore—plus the historic fishing villages, small towns, and the rockets of Wallops Island.

This 90-mile drive can be completed in one day, but the bay and the ocean, the beaches and marshes, the birds and other wildlife, and the quaint towns and other attractions may charm you into spending several days.

The drive begins at the Maryland-Virginia border on four-lane US 13 which follows the high ground 35 to 45 feet above sea level down the middle of the peninsula. The drive meanders back and forth from the Seaside to the Bayside, avoiding US 13 as much as possible, but crossing that highway several times and—when unavoidable—following it for short distances. The meanders and side trips may make the driving directions appear complicated because of the many route numbers, but in most cases road signs will help you to easily find the next town or point of interest.

The drive ends at the southern tip of the peninsula at the Chesapeake Bay Bridge-Tunnel at the mouth of Chesapeake Bay across from Norfolk and Virginia Beach and the starting point for Drive 11.

From the Maryland border on US 13, you pass by flat, sandy farmlands, mixed pine and hardwood forests, plus numerous gas stations, restaurants, and other commercial developments. In 4 miles, at the well-marked signs to Chincoteague, turn left on VA 175.

Early morning fog and drizzle shroud the tidal flats and pine-covered islands along the Wildlife Trail at Chincoteague.

This two-lane road quickly leaves the commercial bustle of US 13 behind. In 5 miles the road curves to the left and passes an airport runway, part of the federal Wallops Flight Center of the National Aeronautics and Space Administration (NASA). On the right is the NASA Visitor Center, unmistakable with the numerous rockets, launchers, and associated space equipment displayed in front. The self-guiding tour inside the visitor center includes scale models of satellites, aircraft, and space vehicles, a moon rock, a space suit, and numerous other exhibits. Because you will retrace this part of the drive, you can visit NASA now or later, when you return from Chincoteague.

The actual launches take place at nearby Wallops Island, which—unfortunately—is not usually open to the public. This facility is not as well known as Cape Canaveral, its big brother in Florida where the space shuttles are launched. Wallops Island is used for small launches, some by private enterprise; since its inception in 1945 it has sent more than 14,000 rockets and satellites into space.

After leaving the NASA facility, VA 175 soon curves to the right and becomes a 4-mile causeway over tidal flats, salt marshes, and water. A bridge over the Chincoteague Channel leads you to Chincoteague Island and the town of Chincoteague (Indian name for "pretty land across the water"), a pleasant resort town with numerous motels, bed-and-breakfast homes, and shops. The town also has several outstanding seafood restaurants where you can experience the gastronomic delights of Chesapeake's famed blue crabs and other sea dishes.

Follow VA 175 through town, turning left on Main Street and then right several blocks later on Maddox Boulevard. On the Chincoteague side of the channel to Assateague Island, you pass the Refuge Waterfowl Museum, known for its displays of duck decoys and exhibits on the art and history of hunting waterfowl. Nearby is the Oyster and Maritime Museum with displays of shells and fossils. Both museums are privately owned and open during the warmer months only.

Cross another short causeway over the Assateague Channel and you arrive at the entrance station to Assateague Island National Seashore and Chincoteague National Wildlife Refuge. The area is administered jointly by two federal agencies of the U.S. Department of the Interior: the National Park Service (Assateague Island National Seashore) and the Fish and Wildlife Service (Chincoteague National Wildlife Refuge). A nominal admission fee is charged. Please note that pets are not allowed on the seashore or refuge, even if they are kept in the vehicle.

What you can do depends in part on how much time you want to spend. The area's many outstanding features and attractions are often overshadowed by its wild horses, made famous by Marguerite Henry's best-selling children's book, *Misty of Chincoteague*. The widely publicized pony roundup and swim

The lighthouse on Assateague Island has been guiding mariners since 1867.

are held the last Wednesday of July. Surplus horses, which have been corralled for the occasion, swim across the channel from Assateague Island to Chincoteague Island. The next day the horses are auctioned off; the average price is about $200. Proceeds benefit the Chincoteague Volunteer Fire Department. This event attracts huge crowds and the heaviest traffic of the year.

The area was established as a wildlife refuge in 1943 to protect the winter feeding grounds of thousands of migratory waterfowl. The entire Atlantic coast of the Eastern Shore—the Seaside—including Chincoteague, lies along the Eastern Flyway, a primary migration route. During spring and fall migrations, millions of birds and hundreds of birders converge on the refuge. Huge flocks of migrating birds on the Eastern Flyway use the marshlands as a stopover on their way north or south. But at any time of year, you will see numerous herons, egrets, and other wading birds, in addition to the waterfowl. Shore birds, including terns, gulls, and sandpipers, reach their peak in July and August; the thickets and forests are home in summer to numerous warblers and other passerine birds. More than 300 species of birds have been spotted in the refuge.

Even a short visit will allow you to see two kinds of deer (Virginia whitetail and the smaller sika elk), an old lighthouse, mile-long stretches of pristine beach, rolling surf, dunes, and quiet marshlands. In addition to birds, the refuge protects several endangered species, including the Delmarva Peninsula fox squirrel, and the nesting grounds of the piping plover.

You may want to walk or hike along the Wildlife Trail or attend a naturalist's talk. Longer hikes away from the developed portions will take you into unspoiled wilderness. Boat trips through the barrier islands and guided wildlife tours are available. Rangers at the entrance station and visitor center can help you plan your visit.

Assateague Island and Assateague Island National Seashore extend 37 miles north into Maryland. The northern tip is operated by the state of Maryland as Assateague State Park, and is adjacent to the towns of Ocean City and Berlin, Maryland.

When you leave the Chincoteague area to continue the drive, head west on VA 175, retracing the route over the causeway and past the NASA Visitor Center and airport. Just past the air base, turn left on VA 798, Atlantic Road.

The drive passes by farms and stands of pines and mixed hardwoods. In a few miles the route number changes to VA 679, but remains Atlantic Avenue. The drive crosses VA 803, which goes to Wallops Island and NASA's rocket launch facility (not open to the public). Continue straight on VA 679, which changes names again to Metompkin Road.

When irrigated, the flat, sandy soil hosts a variety of crops, including cotton, corn, and other vegetables. Virginia Highway 679 changes its name again to Fox Grove Road just before the stop sign and intersection with US 13. Cross over the median of four-lane US 13 and turn left onto the highway.

Railroad buffs will want to take a side trip to the Eastern Shore Railway Museum in the old station at Parksley. The town and museum are a few miles off US 13 to the west on Virginia Highway 176. The museum features several old railcars and railroad exhibits.

The main drive continues on US 13 for about 5 miles to VA 179. Turn right on VA 179 for a short drive to Onancock, Indian name for "foggy place," on the Bayside. Go through town to the wharf and small, picturesque harbor. The wharf is the terminal for the ferry to Tangier Island, an unspoiled village, free of cars, that looks much as it did 50 years ago.

When you leave Onancock, follow VA 179 and watch for signs to VA 178, Savageville Road, a mile or so out of town. Turn right on VA 178, past pine barrens and farmlands.

At Pungoteague, turn left on VA 180. At US 13, VA 180 crosses the median of US 13 and turns left. Go less than a half-mile on US 13 and turn right, still on VA 180. Follow VA 180 to Wachapreague ("town by the sea") on the Seaside. The town, which calls itself the "Flounder Capital of the World," is known for its many charter-fishing and sightseeing boat tours. It is also the home of the College of William and Mary's Eastern Shore Laboratory, known for its ecological and biological studies.

The salt flats, inlets, and barrier islands parallel the shore and stretch for miles into the Atlantic, giving Wachapreague a feeling of openness and grandeur. Most of these remote islands are owned in part or entirely by The Nature Conservancy and make up the Virginia Coast Reserve, which stretches 75 miles from Chincoteague and Wallops Island to Cape Charles at the southern tip of the peninsula.

To continue the drive, turn around and follow VA 180 about a half-mile to VA 605. Turn left on VA 605, passing through more farmlands and pine forest. In 4 miles turn right on VA 182. After crossing some tidal flats, turn left at the intersection with VA 600, a Virginia Scenic Byway.

Tranquil VA 600 passes by woods and farms with occasional views of the bays and offshore islands along the Atlantic side to the left. Virtually all the Atlantic coastline here is preserved as a national wildlife preserve or natural area. Virginia Highway 600 parallels busy US 13 a few miles to east.

Continue on VA 600 about 15 miles to the stop sign at VA 639. Turn right on VA 639 and follow it to a stop sign at Business 13, Bayside Road, in Cheriton. Turn left on Business 13. At the traffic light at US 13, go straight, crossing US 13. The highway number changes to VA 184, Stone Road.

Follow VA 184 to the town of Cape Charles on the Bayside. As you approach town, be sure to admire the water tower cleverly painted to resemble a lighthouse. At one time Cape Charles was the largest town on the peninsula and the southern terminal of the New York, Philadelphia, and Norfolk

Each gull has its own piling at Wachapreague by the low barrier islands on the Seaside of the Eastern Shore.

Railroad. Coal from the mines in the mountains of Virginia and West Virginia was the main cargo. The coal was shipped by rail to Newport News on the southern edge of Chesapeake Bay, transferred to barges for the trip to Cape Charles, and then reloaded on trains headed for Philadelphia, New York, and other cities along the northeastern seaboard. As coal mining and the railroad declined, so did the town.

In recent years many of the fine old homes from the boom years have been renovated, and prosperity is returning. The barge-train ferry still operates, but at a less hectic pace. Several of the restored houses are visible from the boardwalk along the beach overlooking Chesapeake Bay. You can also walk out on the jetty that extends several hundred yards into the water.

When you leave Cape Charles, retrace your steps back to VA 600: Follow VA 184 to US 13 and Business 13. Turn right on VA 639 in Cheriton. At the first intersection with VA 600, turn right (south) to continue the drive.

The peninsula is only a few miles wide at this point, giving you occasional views of the barrier islands, bay, and inlets. Almost at the southern tip is the Eastern Shore of Virginia National Wildlife Refuge, another excellent spot to view birds. During the fall migration, large flocks often rest here for a while before beginning the flight across the bay. To visit this wildlife refuge, turn in at the well-marked sign where VA 600 makes a 90-degree turn to the right about 7 miles from Cheriton.

Until 1984 the mainland section of the Eastern Shore of Virginia National Wildlife Refuge was an Air Force radar station and military installation. All that remain today of that venture are several two-story concrete gun bunkers. These make great observation platforms for bird watching and looking out at the surrounding woodlands, marshes, islands, and nearby Bay Bridge-Tunnel. During fall migration, the bunkers are a favorite spot to observe migrating hawks.

The refuge has a visitor center and some short hiking trails, but the biggest attraction are the birds. The varied habitat supports a large number of species. Check at the visitor center for information.

When you leave the Eastern Shore of Virginia National Wildlife Refuge, turn left on VA 600. That route number ends in about a half-mile at US 13. Turn left on US 13 and continue about a mile to the end of the drive at the Chesapeake Bay Bridge-Tunnel, Drive 11.

For a side trip to Kiptopoke State Park, turn right (north) on US 13 at the stop sign at the end of VA 600. The park is a few miles north on US 13. Turn left into the park entrance on the Bayside. The park is the site of the old ferry terminal used before the Bridge-Tunnel was built. The ferry terminal is being developed as a visitor center. The park has a campground and features nature walkways through the dunes and sandy shores, with excellent bird watching.

11

Chesapeake Bay Bridge-Tunnel
Water, Sun, and Sky

General description: The Chesapeake Bay Bridge-Tunnel is a 23-mile, open-water drive across the mouth of Chesapeake Bay. This highway complex traverses trestles, causeways, bridges, manmade islands, and tunnels to connect the southern tip of the Delmarva Peninsula with the Norfolk-Virginia Beach area.

Special attractions: The views from the bridges and trestles of the open Atlantic and Chesapeake Bay, as you are suspended between sky and water, provide a unique experience. The drive over the water is broken up by two tunnels. A stop at the restaurant and fishing pier 4 miles out at sea on one of the manmade islands gives you the opportunity to walk out over the water to look at birds, ocean-going vessels, and views of the distant shore. Birders consider the manmade islands the best place in Virginia to observe sea birds.

Location: Southeast Virginia between Norfolk and the Eastern Shore (Delmarva Peninsula).

Drive route numbers: U.S. Highway 13.

Travel season: The highway is open year-round. There are occasional fog and rare winter snow. Winter is the best time of year to view sea birds.

Camping: At the northern end of the bridge-tunnel, camping is available at Kiptopoke State Park; the park has 27 tent sites and 94 sites with electric and water hookups. At the southern end of the drive, First Landing/ Seashore State Park in Virginia Beach has more than 200 campsites with facilities from tents to motor homes. Nearby False Cape State Park has a few primitive campsites. Several private campgrounds provide a variety of accommodations in the Norfolk-Virginia Beach area.

Services: The bridge-tunnel has a restaurant and gift shop after the second tunnel. Gasoline is not available. Emergency road service is provided along the entire bridge-tunnel with call boxes every half mile. Gasoline, motels, hotels, and restaurants are available at either end of the drive.

Nearby attractions: The northern end of this drive is the end point for the Eastern Shore (Drive 10). At the southern end of the drive are the beaches of Virginia Beach, and the many attractions of the Norfolk area, including tours of the massive naval base.

Drive 11: Chesapeake Bay Bridge-Tunnel
Water, Sun, and Sky

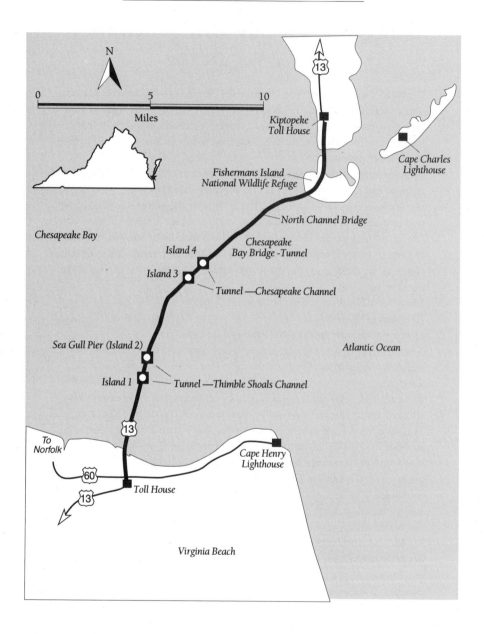

N

0   5   10

Miles

13

Kiptopeke
Toll House

Cape Charles
Lighthouse

Fishermans Island
National Wildlife Refuge

North Channel Bridge

Chesapeake Bay

Chesapeake
Bay Bridge -Tunnel

Island 4

Island 3

Tunnel —Chesapeake Channel

Sea Gull Pier (Island 2)

Atlantic Ocean

Island 1

Tunnel —Thimble Shoals Channel

13

To
Norfolk

Cape Henry
Lighthouse

60

Toll House

13

Virginia Beach

The Iwo Jima Marine War Memorial (Drive 3).

Cabbage along the Blue Ridge Parkway (Drives 6 and 7).

Crabtree Falls in the George Washington National Forest (Drive 1).

The Blue Ridge Parkway offers an excellent view of a log cabin built in the 1890s (Drives 6 and 7).

AA view of Mt. Rogers National Recreation Area from the Appalachian Trail (Drive 21).

The Booker T. Washington National Monument (Drive 6).

Oceanfront along Virginia Beach (Drive 11).

A turkey at the Yorktown Victory Center (Drive 15).

The eternal flame at the John F. Kennedy grave site in Arlington National Cemetery (Drive 3).

The high columns of the riverfront piazza at the Mount Vernon Estate (Drive 3).

Virginia's famous Natural Bridge (Drive 12).

The Drive

This 23-mile drive follows U.S. Highway 13 across the Chesapeake Bay Bridge-Tunnel at the mouth of Chesapeake Bay, connecting the Eastern Shore of Virginia with the Norfolk-Virginia Beach area. Its 17.6 miles of bridges, tunnels, causeways, trestled roadways, and manmade islands make this the world's longest bridge-tunnel complex. Its two mile-long tunnels, two bridges, 12 miles of trestled roads, four manmade islands, and 2 miles of causeway, plus 5.5 miles of approach road make for a unique driving experience.

The drive offers superb views of Chesapeake Bay and the open Atlantic Ocean. It includes a stop 3 miles out at sea, where Chesapeake Bay meets the Atlantic Ocean, at a restaurant and 625-foot fishing pier on one of the manmade islands. You can walk out on the pier for a more leisurely view of the water, or look for passing ships while enjoying a bite at the Sea Gull Pier Restaurant. The at-sea location also makes this the best place in Virginia to watch sea birds.

Weather and time of day make this drive a varied experience. Although it is a four-season drive, ice and snow can make it hazardous in winter. Occasional fog, primarily in spring and fall, can give you a feeling of isolation as you drive along cocooned in your vehicle. On clear, moonless nights, distant lights from shore and passing ships contrast with the black of the water and the pinpoints of starlight; a full moon can light up the phosphorescent sea almost as brilliantly as day.

The mouth of Chesapeake Bay is one of the busiest maritime areas in the world, and you see a lot of its activity from the bridge-tunnel. From the huge naval bases around Norfolk, aircraft carriers, battleships, submarines, and other vessels of war come and go on their military missions. At the railheads in Hampton and Newport News, coal trains from mines in the mountains of Virginia, West Virginia, and Pennsylvania are loaded onto seagoing barges for delivery to ports all over the world. Tankers and cargo vessels carry products and goods of all kinds to and from Baltimore, Richmond, Washington, D.C., and other ports along Chesapeake Bay and the James, Potomac, and Rappahannock Rivers. All of this traffic must cross over or under the Chesapeake Bay Bridge-Tunnel.

Early travelers going to or from the Eastern Shore had to go overland through parts of Maryland from the north or use some kind of water transport from the west and south. Since colonial days, private ferry boats provided the main means of access; as automobile travel grew in the 1900s, a vehicle-carrying ferry became an integral link of US 13.

In the 1950s it became apparent that a replacement for the existing ferry system was needed. The Virginia legislature appointed a commission to study the possible construction of a bridge-tunnel. The project was approved, and the original two-lane highway was open to traffic in 1964.

As traffic increased, plans were made to construct a parallel causeway to make a four-lane roadway. This parallel structure was opened in 1999. The tunnels will remain two-lane for now, but future plans include expanding them to four lanes as well.

The drive can be made in either direction, but is described here from north to south. It can easily be combined with Drive 10, the Eastern Shore. Allow a minimum of an hour and a half for the total drive; this includes the actual driving time of about 45 minutes and time for a stopover at the island restaurant, pier, and gift shop. If you stop to fish or bird watch, your trip may take considerably longer.

The drive begins at US 13 at the North Toll Plaza on the approach to the bridge-tunnel. The toll for passenger cars in 1999 was $10. After crossing a short bridge, the drive passes through Fishermans Island National Wildlife Refuge. This refuge supports diverse colonies of nesting water birds, including several species of gulls, terns, herons, and ibis. Almost 300 species of birds have been identified on the refuge. However, to protect the birds, the refuge can be visited only by special permit, and stops are not allowed.

Open water beckons on the trestle beyond Fishermans Island. To the right lies Chesapeake Bay; to the left is the Atlantic Ocean. In a few miles

An aerial view shows the twin roadways curving away from Fishermans Island to cross the open waters of Chesapeake Bay. The first tunnel appears dimly in the distance.
CHESAPEAKE BAY BRIDGE AND TUNNEL DISTRICT PHOTO

you cross the North Channel Bridge, 80 feet above the water and the highest point on the structure. This bridge provides passage underneath for small craft going to and from the Eastern Shore. Go slowly, and enjoy the vista of open water reaching to the horizon around you.

Unless the fog is heavy, as you drive down the far side of the bridge, you can see the highway, islands, and tunnel portals stretching to Norfolk and the southern shore about 15 miles ahead.

In 1965, the year after the original bridge-tunnel was open, it was selected as one of the "Seven Engineering Wonders of the Modern World" and, in competition with more than 100 other projects, it was recognized by the American Society of Civil Engineers as an "Outstanding Civil Engineering Achievement."

The Chesapeake Bay Bridge-Tunnel was officially named the "Lucius J. Kellam, Jr. Bridge-Tunnel" in 1987. Kellam was chairman of the original tunnel commission and its predecessor, the ferry commission, from 1954 to 1993, and it was his foresight and leadership that helped make the structure a reality.

In a few miles you come to the first of four manmade islands built on tons of rocks that were carried by barge to the site. (This island is actually Island 4, because the islands are numbered from south to north.) The islands provide approaches to the tunnels and house the ventilation equipment.

The islands are also the best places in Virginia to observe sea birds. These rock piles provide abundant feeding grounds for fish, shellfish, and other aquatic life, and these in turn attract diving sea ducks and other birds. The only island normally open to the public is the last one on our trip—the Sea Gull Pier Restaurant Island after the second tunnel.

Birders (and the curious) can visit the other islands if they obtain written permission in advance. Write or call the Chesapeake Bay Bridge and Tunnel District before your trip, and they will send you written permission and instructions to stop at the other islands. (See the Appendix for the address and phone number. Allow the district office at least two weeks to receive and process your request.) Do not stop without permission; you will receive a ticket and fine.

Bird life is most abundant in the winter months. Water birds include all three species of scoters, plus many other ducks and gulls. Snow buntings, ruddy turnstones, and double-crested and great cormorants are commonly seen. The birding is best when the weather is at its worst: during January and February after a hard freeze has iced over the tidal creeks and inlets of the mainland.

At Island 4 the drive enters the mile-long Chesapeake Channel Tunnel which allows shipping traffic from Chesapeake Bay to pass overhead. The tunnels are still two-lane; new tunnels were not included when the parallel roadways were constructed. Originally, bridges were considered instead of tunnels for the shipping channels, but U.S. Navy officials objected because bridges, no matter how high, would restrict the height of naval vessels passing under them, and sabotage to the bridges could block the water passage completely.

You emerge from the Chesapeake Channel Tunnel at Island 3, about the halfway point on the drive, and 8 miles from land in either direction. The drive continues over low-level trestles for several miles to Island 2, the portal for the Thimble Shoals Channel Tunnel. The channel over this tunnel is the main shipping lane for the U.S. Navy Atlantic fleet and the ports at Norfolk, Portsmouth, Newport News, and Hampton.

When you exit from this tunnel, make a sharp right turn at the sign to visit the public facilities at the Sea Gull Pier and Restaurant on Island 1. The pier extends 625 feet into Chesapeake Bay, with scenic views of the Norfolk-Virginia Beach shoreline 4 miles away. The pier can be crowded on summer weekends when local anglers try their luck at catching bluefish, trout, flounder, shark, and other species. Bait and tackle are available.

Look back over the Chesapeake Channel toward Island 2. Because this is such a busy shipping channel, you stand a good chance of seeing a sub-

A freighter heads for port as it crosses the tunnel by the Sea Gull Pier. The island and ventilation building at the far side of the tunnel are to the left of the ship.

Anglers test their luck while others sightsee on 625-foot-long Sea Gull Pier, 4 miles from shore.

marine, aircraft carrier, or freighter slowly making its way to or from port, floating over the tunnel you recently drove through. Sunsets (and sunrises) over the water can be spectacular, and the bird watching can be rewarding. From the restaurant you can enjoy watching the water while having a complete meal or just a cup of coffee. A small gift shop provides souvenirs. Gasoline and auto services are not available.

A thousand feet beneath the waters and underlying sediments of Chesapeake Bay, geologists have found evidence of an ancient impact structure, most probably a bolide (meteor) crater. Based on the age of the surrounding sediments, this event occurred in late Eocene time, some 40 million years ago (and 25 million years after the demise of the dinosaurs).

As you leave the pier, turn right onto the roadway toward the distant shore. Ahead lies Norfolk to the right and Virginia Beach to the left. From the pier it is about 4 miles over causeways to the end of the drive at the South Toll Plaza, located halfway between Norfolk and Virginia Beach.

You should have your next destination in mind as you leave the toll plaza. Well-marked signs will help direct you to connecting roads and interstates, including I-64, I-264, I-564, I-664, US 13, US 17, and US 60, and the surrounding cities of Norfolk, Virginia Beach, Portsmouth, Hampton, Newport News, and Williamsburg.

12

Goshen Pass and Lake Moomaw
Lexington to Covington

General description: This is a mountain drive west of Lexington with a variety of scenic and historic sites. It passes the Virginia Horse Center, and goes by the steep cliffs and rushing streams of Goshen Pass in Jefferson National Forest. From there, it heads down the valley of Bath County, past numerous hot springs and spas, including the well-known Homestead resort. Other features of the drive include Falling Spring Falls, first described by Thomas Jefferson, and imposing Gathright Dam and Lake Moomaw in the heart of Jefferson National Forest. The drive is almost 65 miles long and ends at Covington.

Special attractions: Goshen Pass, Lake Moomaw, Homestead, Falling Spring Falls.

Location: West-central Virginia. Lexington is at Exit 188 of Interstate 81.

Drive route numbers: U.S. Highways 11 and 220; Virginia Highways 39, 640, 687, and 666; and local Forest Service roads.

Travel season: The drive can be made at any time of year; but roads may be temporarily closed by snow during the winter months. Summer is the most popular travel season. Spring brings the colorful blossoms of redbud, rhododendron, dogwood, and other flowering plants, while in autumn the changing leaves bathe the hillsides in yellow, orange, and red.

Camping: On the drive itself, Lake Moomaw in Jefferson National Forest has several hundred tent campsites scattered around the lake and forest; some are wilderness sites, but most are equipped with showers and electricity. Nearby, but off the drive route, Douthat State Park has 116 campsites, many with all the amenities, that can accommodate everything from tent campers to motor homes. Two private campgrounds near Natural Bridge have about 300 campsites, most with full hookups.

Services: Motels, restaurants, and gasoline can be found in Lexington and Covington at either end of the ride. Lodging, meals, and gasoline are available at Hot Springs; accommodations range from the sumptuous Homestead to simple motels. Nearby Douthat State Park has about 30 rental cabins.

Nearby attractions: Douthat State Park, nestled between mountain ridges, features camping, hiking, fishing, and boating. Heavily advertised Natural Bridge, south of Lexington on US 11, is a 215-foot-high limestone arch.

Drive 12: Goshen Pass and Lake Moomaw

Lexington to Covington

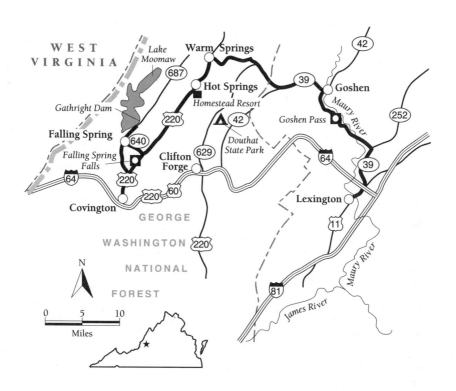

 The Drive

The drive starts in downtown Lexington, a beautiful and historic cultural center. After leaving Lexington, you soon pass the Virginia Horse Center, where equestrian events are held year-round, and enter Goshen Pass in Jefferson National Forest, known for its steep rock cliffs that rise abruptly from the banks of the Maury River. The drive then traverses Bath County, whose hot springs and spas have been popular since colonial days, including the Homestead, a well-known resort. Other features of the drive include Falling Spring Falls and Gathright Dam at Lake Moomaw in the heart of the national forest. The drive ends in Covington.

Lexington is home to both Washington and Lee University and Virginia Military Institute. Although both schools share a military history, their

Steeply dipping limestone rises above the rushing Maury River in Goshen Pass.

adjacent campuses are an architectural contrast: Washington and Lee's stately colonial- and federal-style buildings, reminiscent of Virginia's genteel traditions, sit across from VMI's angular and sober gothic constructions.

Well-known military figures have been associated with both schools. Confederate General Robert E. Lee assumed presidency of Washington and Lee (then known as Washington College) six months after the close of the Civil War at Appomattox. Before the Civil War, Confederate General Stonewall Jackson instructed VMI students in the tactics and strategy of battle. General George C. Patton, who fought in both World War I and World War II and later devised the Marshall Plan to rehabilitate Europe, graduated from VMI.

The visitor center downtown can provide you with suggestions for and directions to other nearby attractions, including the Stonewall Jackson House, the George C. Marshall Museum, and museums at VMI. If you get tired of military exhibits, visit the Cyrus McCormick Farm, maintained to look much as it did in the 1830s when McCormick revolutionized agriculture with the invention of the mechanical reaper.

To begin the drive, from downtown Lexington take US 11 north. Cross Interstate 64 just outside of town and turn left in a quarter mile on two-lane VA 39, a Virginia Scenic Byway. In a few minutes you pass the Virginia Horse Center, one of the country's largest equestrian facilities. Events are held all year, and include competitions as diverse as grand prix jumping and walking horse races, to horse-judging shows and auctions. The horse festival in April features all of these. The Center includes a 4,000-seat coliseum (for people) and more than 700 stables (for horses).

As the winding Maury River Road crosses the Shenandoah Valley, you are virtually surrounded by mountains. Behind are the peaks of the Blue Ridge Mountains; ahead, where you are going, are the rounded slopes of the Allegheny Mountains. The road's namesake—the Maury River—appears on the left.

About 12 miles from Lexington, VA 39 follows the Maury River into the George Washington National Forest and the towering cliffs of Goshen Pass. For several miles you wind past 1,000-foot-high cliffs of steeply dipping limestone and sandstone that tower over the boulders in the bed of the rushing river. Rhododendron, dogwood, and redbud grow to the roadside amid maples, pines, and hemlocks. Several scenic turnouts and roadside parks give picnickers, anglers, canoeists, swimmers, and tube riders access to the water.

After several miles you emerge from the pass into a little valley. As you drive through the small town of Goshen you can see the Calf Pasture River on the right where VA 42 merges with VA 39.

Continue on VA 39. A few miles past Goshen the drive enters another river pass, more narrow but less spectacular than Goshen Pass. This one follows the Cow Pasture River (a little bigger than the Calf Pasture River).

In a few miles you pass VA 629 which leads to Douthat State Park, a popular camping and picnicking area. Virginia Highway 39 leaves the river valley to begin the winding climb over the ridge of Warm Springs Mountain, elevation 2,950 feet.

The road descends from the ridge to the intersection of US 220 at Warm Springs, county seat of Bath County, where there are several public spas and baths. The town and the county get their name from the numerous hot springs that issue from the fractured limestone of the valley floor. The springs here have a temperature of about 99 degrees F.

In town is the site of Terrill Hill, home of two brothers, both generals, and both killed during the Civil War. They served on opposing sides. On the Union side, Brigadier General William R. Terrill, a graduate of West Point, was killed in 1862 during a skirmish in Perry, Kentucky. His Confederate brother, Brigadier General James B. Terrill, a graduate of VMI, died during the Battle of the Wilderness in 1864 near Fredericksburg. Legend says that their grieving father erected a monument to his sons saying, "God alone knows which was right."

Turn left on US 220, which follows the valley floor. You will see remains of several bathhouses and resorts, most of which are now closed. One that is still open, and is still a major resort, is the huge and imposing Homestead at Hot Springs. The first bathhouse here was designed by Thomas

The 1,310-foot-long earth-and-rock Gathright Dam rises 250 feet above the Jackson River. The drive crosses the top of the dam.

Jefferson in 1761. The original Homestead opened as an inn in 1768. Today's Homestead features more than 600 guest rooms and suites; in addition to 105-degree mineral baths and spa, it offers tennis, three golf courses, skeet and target shooting, other sports, some ten restaurants, and even ice skating and downhill skiing in season.

Continue on US 220, past the Homestead's verdant golf courses. About 8 miles from Hot Springs and about 200 feet past the large rocks at VA 640 are an overlook and small parking area on the right from which to view Falling Spring Falls. Use caution because the turnoff is easy to miss. The falls, first described by Thomas Jefferson in 1798, form lacy cascades dropping about 200 feet.

After you view the falls, turn around and drive back 200 feet to VA 640. Turn left on VA 640, a narrow, two-lane road, toward the town of Falling Spring. At Falling Spring turn right on VA 687.

At the small store and intersection, make an acute left turn on the unnumbered Forest Service road at the sign to Lake Moomaw and Gathright Dam. Cross the Jackson River and make a sharp right turn on VA 600 at another Lake Moomaw sign. (The road names and numbers are poorly marked or missing, but the signs pointing to Lake Moomaw are clear and unambiguous.)

You'll have several views of Lake Moomaw and pass the visitor center before reaching Gathright Dam itself. The dam, with the road on top of it, is an earth-and-rock structure about 1,310 feet long, rising 250 feet above the Jackson River. On the other side of the dam, the road makes a loop several miles long with numerous views of the lake with mountains rising from the far shore. You pass several swimming, boating, and fishing areas.

The dam was built in 1965 because of fear of floods downstream in Covington. The lake has 43 miles of shoreline and covers about 2,500 acres. Today the lake, with its surrounding wildlife management area, is popular with anglers, swimmers, boaters, bird watchers, and hikers. It is known for its large wild turkey population, and has several bald eagle nesting areas. There are half a dozen campsites and campgrounds scattered around the area.

"Moomaw" may sound like an ancient Indian name, but the lake is named for Benjamin C. Moomaw, Jr. An executive director of the Covington-Allegheny Chamber of Commerce, Moomaw, with landowner-sportsman Thomas M. Gathright, pushed for construction of the dam for flood control purposes.

When you leave the dam, retrace your route to the intersection in Natural Well and turn right on VA 687. Stay on VA 687 past Falling Spring (don't turn on VA 640) to the intersection in several miles with US 220. Turn right on US 220 into Covington where the drive ends. The large plant you see as you approach Covington belongs to the West Virginia Paper Company.

Follow signs to I-64 to head east back to Lexington or west to the West Virginia border.

The Homestead has been entertaining guests since 1768. Today's guests may be more interested in golf than mineral baths, but the emphasis is still on service and comfort.

13

Lee's Retreat

Petersburg to Appomattox

General description: Lee's Retreat is a 50-mile, historical drive that traces the closing days of the Civil War as Union General Ulysses S. Grant relentlessly pursued Confederate General Robert E. Lee to Lee's surrender at Appomattox. The drive crosses much of the rural Piedmont area of central Virginia with numerous stops at historical or military points of interest.

Special attractions: The main attractions are the historical stops which feature short, interpretive radio broadcasts. Sailor's Creek Battlefield Historical State Park is the scene of the last major battle of the war. Appomattox Court House National Historic Park, where Lee surrendered to Grant, has been restored to look as it did in 1865. The drive passes through Appomattox-Buckingham State Forest and near two state parks.

Location: Central Virginia, west of Petersburg.

Drive route numbers: Virginia Highways 708, 153, 38, 671, 642, 617, 618, 619, 45, 657, 600, 653, 638, 636, and 24; U.S. Highways 360, 460, and Business 460. The route is complicated, but all turns and stops are well marked by special "Lee's Retreat" signs.

Travel season: All year.

Camping: Camping in season is available at Holliday Lake State Park, a few miles from the main drive.

Services: Gasoline, restaurants, motels, and hotels are available in Petersburg and Farmville. Appomattox has restaurants, gasoline, and some motels.

Nearby attractions: Petersburg at the start of the drive has numerous historic sites, including Petersburg National Battlefield, the Siege Museum, and the Pamplin Park Civil War Site.

 The Drive

Lee's Retreat traces the ending days of the Civil War in April 1865. It follows Confederate General Robert E. Lee's route as his Army of Northern Virginia was pursued by Union General Ulysses S. Grant's Army of the Potomac from Petersburg to Lee's surrender at Appomattox Court House, effectively ending the Civil War. The route is a winding one, primarily on narrow, two-lane roads. Lee's Retreat is one of several Civil War motor trails designed and established by the Virginia Civil War Trails; this private organization works with the state and local communities to preserve Civil War

Drive 13: Lee's Retreat
Petersburg to Appomattox

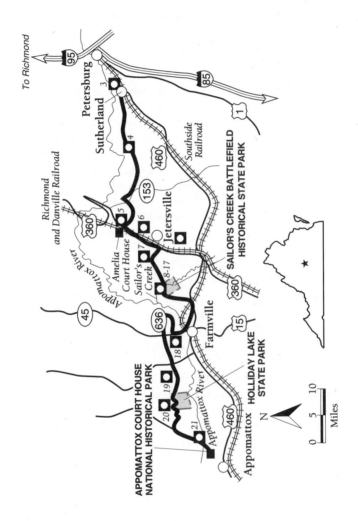

sites and make them accessible to the public. Most of the drive is also a designated Virginia Scenic Byway. (Grant and Lee met several times in battle outside Fredericksburg before Lee retreated south to Petersburg. These conflicts are described in Drive 8.)

The drive lies in the Piedmont area of the state between the Coastal Plain to the east and the Blue Ridge to the west. The Piedmont here is characterized by gently rolling hills, thick, fertile soil, farmlands that have been cultivated since colonial days, and extensive second-growth forests. The drive gives you a good look from back roads at the rural, mostly unspoiled land of the Piedmont, much of which is little changed since the Civil War. It passes through the Appomattox-Buckingham State Forest and by two state parks.

The route is twisty with numerous route changes because it is laid out from a historical point of view and to stop at points of interest. It is easy to follow, however, because of the well-marked "Lee's Retreat" signs that are found along the route. At each stop is an informative display and a short, interpretive AM-radio broadcast that you can listen to on your car radio.

Because the drive is well marked, and to avoid cluttering up the description with numerous route changes, minimal road directions are given here. The numbered stops in the text refer to corresponding numbers on the book's map and to the sites designated by the Virginia Civil War Trails.

Lee's rear guard was attacked by Union cavalry troops at Namozine Church. After the confrontation, the church was used as a hospital.

This drive covers that portion of Lee's Retreat from Sutherland Station (stop 3) to Appomattox Court House (stop 21).

Free maps of Lee's Retreat, which give more detail than the one in this book, can be obtained in advance by calling one of the numbers in the Appendix; maps are also available at many historical sites and other places in Petersburg.

Before starting you may want to visit some of the Civil War sites in Petersburg, particularly if your knowledge of the Civil War is minimal. The visitor center at South Side Railroad Station can get you oriented. The Siege Museum and Petersburg National Battlefield tell the story of Grant's nine-and-a-half-month blockade and siege of the city when he slowly surrounded Petersburg and cut off Lee's supply lines from the south. After a final assault on April 2, 1865, at what is now the privately owned Pamplin Park Civil War Site, Union forces broke through Lee's line defending Petersburg. That night Lee abandoned Petersburg and headed west with his bedraggled Confederate forces, some 80,000 hungry and weary soldiers and a wagon train of supplies and equipment grudgingly pulled by ribs-thin horses.

The drive begins west of Petersburg at Sutherland (stop 3) where VA 708 leads west from US 460. Here Grant cut off the South Side Railroad, Lee's only remaining supply line into Petersburg.

Virginia Highway 708 traverses gently rolling forest and farmland. At one time thick stands of hardwoods and pines covered the area. Early settlers soon found that the thick, almost rock-free soil grew rich, abundant crops, so that by the time of the Civil War the majority of the land was under cultivation. Tobacco, the main crop, provided the economic backbone and support for Virginia and the Confederate Army. Tobacco is still important today, but you will also see in season, fields of soybeans, corn, wheat, and other crops.

Traveling mostly at night to avoid Union troops, Lee retreated toward Amelia Court House where he had arranged for food and supplies to arrive by railroad. From there, he planned to take his troops from both Richmond and Petersburg to North Carolina to join other Confederate forces.

Union cavalry troops attacked Lee's retreating and lagging rear guard at Namozine Church (stop 4), which was used as a hospital after the confrontation. The church, built in 1847, is still standing today.

About 18 miles from Sutherland, turn right on VA 153 (this turn, like all of them, is well marked). Turn left in 3 miles on VA 38. Follow the route to Amelia Court House (stop 5) on US 360 where the Richmond and Danville Railroad parallel the highway. When Lee arrived here, there was no train and no supplies, so he turned south toward North Carolina. On the court house lawn (a block off the main drive) is an imposing memorial to Confederate soldiers.

At Jetersville (stop 6) Lee encountered more Union troops, which forced him to abandon his plans to go to North Carolina. Instead he headed west to Farmville, hoping to find food and supplies for his impoverished army, marching at night to avoid Grant's forces.

But the Union forces kept attacking Lee's strung-out rear guard, with minor skirmishes at Amelia Springs (stop 7) and Deatonville (stop 8). At Holt's Corner (stop 9), now the junction of VA 617 and VA 618, the main portion of Lee's army went straight (along VA 618) to cross Saylor's (or Sailor's) Creek, while a wagon train went north (VA 617).

Saylor's Creek was the final major battle of the Civil War. As Lee's army struggled to cross the bogs and mud of the creek, Grant's Union forces, nearly 100,000 strong, caught up with them. Overpowered, some 7,000 Confederate soldiers were killed, and about 8,000 surrendered.

This battle scene is preserved in Sailor's Creek Battlefield Historical State Park (stop 9—Holt's Corner—and stops 10 and 11). Today the drive curves down to a small creek through thick woods, a pleasant change from the nearly flat farmlands that give no hint of its bloody history. Interpretive services are available at the park during the warmer months, but it can be visited all year.

From the creek bottom the drive reverses and retraces the route to the intersection with VA 618, passing the Lockett House (stop 12), which still has bullet holes from the battle. The Confederate wagon train that went north was attacked as it crossed Saylor's Creek at Double Bridges (stop 13). Remains of the bridges can be seen on the left.

At Rice's Depot (stop 14) the drive heads toward Farmville on four-lane US 460. The Confederates captured several hundred Union troops (stop 15) who attempted to burn the railroad structure over the Appomattox River, but none of this is visible from the site.

Follow the drive into Farmville. The city today is an agricultural and carpet-manufacturing center, and the site of Longwood College. In 1865 it was a tobacco-growing town of 1,500, and many residents watched fearfully as both armies passed through the area.

In the center of town turn right on VA 45 (Main Street). Ahead you will see a few carpet mills in some old brick buildings. Turn left into the parking lot by the banks of the Appomattox River (stop 16, Farmville). The supply train Lee was hoping for did not appear. He crossed the Appomattox River and headed north.

Continue north on VA 45. As you cross the river, you will see the current railroad bridge over the river. At Cumberland Church (stop 17) Union troops attacked, delaying Lee's march north.

Turn right on VA 657. Confederate troops burned four spans of High Bridge (stop 18), but the lower wagon bridge remained, so Grant's troops were able to cross the river and continue their pursuit of Lee. Unfortunately there is no view of the river or the bridge from this spot.

Turn left on VA 600, and left again in about 2 miles on VA 653. The drive heads west, crosses VA 45 and becomes VA 636. Lee also turned west, and followed this exact route.

In 7 miles the drive crosses US 15. At Clifton (stop 19) on April 8, Grant received a letter from Lee suggesting a peace meeting. Grant left the next morning and rode into Appomattox Court House.

For several miles the drive passes through the Appomattox-Buckingham State Forest, which has extensive stands of second growth of Southern Pine and hardwoods. Nearby, and within the forest, is Holliday Lake State Park. A small lake in the park provides fishing, boating, and swimming. There are 30 campsites. Several archeological sites within and near the park give evidence that early man lived here some 8,000 years ago.

At New Store (stop 20) Lee's army was still being pursued by Grant's troops. Lee turned south toward Appomattox Court House. The drive turns left on VA 24, about 5 miles beyond this stop, and heads south toward Appomattox.

In 3 miles you pass Confederate General Longstreet's soldiers' hastily built breastworks (chest-high lines of earth—stop 21) to protect Lee's rear troops, but most of his weary army had already reached Appomattox Court House 4 miles south.

A park ranger discusses the Civil War with several reenactors in authentic garb outside the restored Clover Hill Tavern at Appomattox Court House National Historic Park.

Visitors climb the steps of the McLean House where Grant and Lee signed the terms of surrender ending four years of fighting.

Turn right into Appomattox Court House National Historic Park. On April 8, 1865, Lee surrendered his men to Grant. The official surrender took place the next day when Robert E. Lee, commanding general of the Army of Northern Virginia, surrendered to Ulysses S. Grant, commander of the Army of the Potomac and general-in-chief of all United States forces.

The surrender ceremony took place in the home of Wilmer McLean. Among the many paradoxes of the Civil War is that McLean, a civilian, was an unwilling observer at both the beginning and the end of the war. Originally he lived in Manassas, where he and his family witnessed the First Battle of Manassas. To ensure his family's safety, McLean moved with them to Appomattox Court House where he believed they would be out of danger and far removed from further conflict.

At the surrender ceremony April 12, Grant's soldiers stood at attention, rifles at present arms, honoring and saluting their former Confederate foes as Lee's 28,000 remaining soldiers laid down their rifles. The Confederate soldiers received written paroles enabling them to safely return to their homes.

Four years of Civil War, fought primarily on Virginia soil, resulted in approximately 630,000 deaths and more than one million casualties. Some units had been fighting for the full four years and their ranks were literally decimated. For example, the 6th Louisiana Volunteers started with almost

1,000 eager recruits in New Orleans in 1861; 55 of them survived to receive their paroles at Appomattox Court House.

The village of Appomattox Court House has been rebuilt to look as it did in 1865, including shops and stores and the McLean House where the surrender was signed. Exhibits, guided tours, and reenactments help tell the complex story of this vital part of Virginia and United States history.

The drive ends here, although Lee's Retreat continues to nearby Appomattox and additional stops. Although Appomattox is best known for its role in the Civil War, it is also the birthplace of Joel Walker Sweeney, inventor of the five-string banjo in 1831.

14

The Plantation Road

The Colonial James River

General description: This 55-mile drive follows the winding Plantation Road along the James River from Richmond to Williamsburg. In colonial days this was the center of commerce for the state, and the James River was the main means of travel. Well-to-do farmers and statesmen built mansions and plantations along the river. The drive follows the inland plantation route, passing by several restored colonial plantations that you can visit. In addition to the plantations, the drive passes through wooded groves, rich farmland, and tidewater inlets.

Special attractions: The numerous colonial mansions and plantations along the James River are of primary interest. Most are lovingly restored and furnished, including grounds and gardens, and provide guided tours of the buildings and grounds. Other attractions include Fort Harrison, a part of Richmond National Battlefield Park, which played a crucial role in the Battle of Richmond, and a side trip to a national fish hatchery.

Location: East-central Virginia between Richmond and Williamsburg.

Drive route numbers: The drive follows Virginia Highway 5 with short side trips or turnoffs on Virginia Highways 106/156, 608, 633, and 658.

Travel season: All year. Most plantations are open daily except for some major holidays such as Christmas. The warmer months attract large crowds.

Camping: The closest campgrounds are at Jamestown, a few miles from the southern end of the drive. They are privately operated.

Services: All services are available at the Richmond and Williamsburg ends of the drive, and occasionally along the drive. Several bed-and-breakfast establishments and restaurants are scattered over the drive.

Nearby attractions: The capital city of Richmond and historic Williamsburg at either end of the drive offer a variety of attractions. See Drive 15, Colonial Parkway, for a complete description of the Williamsburg-Jamestown-Yorktown area.

 ## The Drive

That part of Virginia along the James River between Richmond and Williamsburg is some of the most historical in the country. In the early 1600s it was the site of the first westward expansion of English-speaking America, and its valuable agricultural products, particularly tobacco, helped make the Virginia colonies a most important economic and political power.

Drive 14: The Plantation Road

The Colonial James River

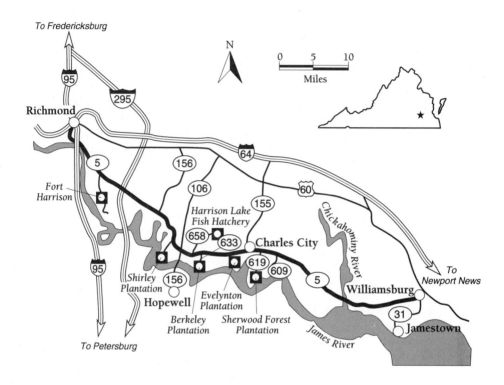

Dominating this economy were several large plantations along the James River, each one essentially a self-supporting community and farmland.

The plantations themselves are gone, but many manor houses, mansions, and outbuildings remain, restored to their colonial splendor, privately owned, and open to the public. They are all listed on the National Register of Historic Places; most are also National Historic Landmarks and Virginia Historic Landmarks. They have survived more than 300 years of social, civil, and technological change, including depressions and booms, the Revolutionary War, War of 1812, the Civil War, and Reconstruction. Because they are privately owned, all must charge a fee to obtain needed funds for their preservation, upkeep, and maintenance.

The region has remained rural, with extensive woods and forests, river and tidal lands, and bountiful farmlands, despite its long history of settlement and its proximity to the colonial capitals of Jamestown and Williamsburg, and to Richmond, the Confederate and state capital.

This drive follows the Plantation Road, VA 5, along the northern bank of the James River from the outskirts of Richmond to Williamsburg. It begins east of Richmond at Exit 22 of Interstate 295 where it crosses VA 5. You can also begin the drive from downtown Richmond by following VA 5.

The 55-mile-long drive begins near the Fort Harrison section of Richmond National Battlefield Park. Fort Harrison, part of a necklace of Confederate forts surrounding Richmond, was captured by General Ulysses S. Grant's troops in September 1864. This crucial battle led to the loss of Richmond, the Confederate capital, several months later. Fourteen Black Union soldiers were awarded the Medal of Honor for their bravery during the battle.

To visit Fort Harrison, from the intersection at I-295 go north (toward Richmond) on VA 5 about 2 miles to an unnumbered road at the park entrance and turn left. This section of the battlefield park contains miles of Confederate breastworks (trenches) that surrounded and protected Richmond. The visitor center will provide maps and information.

If you don't want to visit Fort Harrison, from the intersection at I-295 go south (toward Williamsburg) on VA 5. The two-lane, winding road passes by wooded farmland. Because you are driving down the valley of the James River, the land is fairly flat. This unpresumptuous road has several names that you may notice from signs: Plantation Road, New Market Road, and the John Tyler Memorial Highway. Soon you enter Charles City County.

In a few miles you come to VA 608 and the entrance to Shirley Plantation on the right. Like all the plantations, this one was built to front on the main highway of colonial times, the James River. Rivers were the lifeblood of the early settlers, providing the swiftest and safest means of transportation between Richmond, Williamsburg, and the open ocean.

Trees meet in an arch over the entrance roadway. Shirley Plantation has belonged to the Hill-Carter family since 1611 and is still occupied by the 10th and 11th generation of that group. The mansion, built in 1724, was known for its many modern and innovative features. The most dramatic and best known of these is the flying, or hanging, staircase in the main hallway, which ascends to the second floor with no support beams. Another modern feature was indoor running water made possible by a cistern in the attic. Although water had to be carried up to the cistern, it cut down on broken dishes because the dishes could be washed in the parlor instead of carrying them outside.

Return to VA 5 and turn right. In less than a mile you come to the intersection with VA 106/156. An optional right turn on VA 106/156 will take you across the James River on a free drawbridge. This high span will give you a better view of the river, 2 miles wide at this point, than you can get from VA 5 or any of the plantations. At the other end of the bridge, go to the stop sign at VA 10, where you can turn around and cross the bridge again to rejoin VA 5, and turn right.

Century-old trees shield historic Berkeley Plantation, home of two presidents: William Henry Harrison and his grandson Benjamin Harrison.

In a few miles VA 658 leads left to the Harrison Lake National Fish Hatchery. The hatchery has several ponds where you can see hatchlings, a short nature trail, and an observation platform for observing egrets and shore birds. The lake is locally popular for boating and fishing.

Return to VA 5 and turn left. In a few miles you come to VA 633, the turnoff for Berkeley Plantation, the most historic of all the plantations.

Its European history began when 38 settlers from England came ashore here on December 4, 1619, and celebrated the first Thanksgiving in America, two years before the Pilgrims arrived at Plymouth Rock, Massachusetts. A reenactment of this event is held the first Sunday of November each year, near a replica of the ship afloat in the James. The early settlers are also credited with distilling the first bourbon. This brew, made from corn liquor, reputedly proved far more popular than their weak English ale.

Berkeley is one of only two houses in the United States that is the ancestral home of two presidents plus a signer of the Declaration of Independence. (The other is the Adams house near Boston, Massachusetts.) The Berkeley property was acquired by the Harrison family in 1691, and the main house was constructed in 1726 by Benjamin Harrison IV. It was his son, Benjamin Harrison V, who became a signer of the Declaration of Independence. His son, William Henry Harrison, who was born here in 1773, was elected the ninth president in 1840. This election was the first time campaign buttons and banners were used; many are on display in the mansion.

The president-elect spent many hours at his desk in the mansion composing his inaugural address. Unfortunately, the address took two hours to deliver on a raw, rainy day in 1841. Following the speech the new president contracted pneumonia, and he died after just one month in office. He was succeeded in office by his vice president and neighbor, John Tyler, who lived at nearby Sherwood Forest Plantation, which you will pass later in this drive. The other Harrison president who lived here was Benjamin Harrison, William Henry Harrison's grandson, who became the 23rd president in 1888.

During the Civil War the plantation was the headquarters for Union General George McClellan and his 140,000 troops of the Army of the Potomac who camped here in 1862. President Lincoln conferred here with McClellan several times. And here the poignant notes of the bugle call "Taps," a memento to those killed in battle, was composed and heard for the first time, echoing over the James, during the encampment.

In addition to the house and authentic furnishings, there are 10 acres of formal, terraced boxwood gardens and lawn extending from the house to the James River. Shrines to "Taps" and the first Thanksgiving are near the ship replica on the river.

Return to VA 5 and turn right. In a few miles you pass Evelynton Plantation. The plantation was home to Edmund Ruffin, the Confederate known for firing the first shot of the Civil War at Fort Sumpter. The mansion was burned during the Civil War. It was restored and open to the public in 1985.

Continue on VA 5 to the county seat in Charles City where you can see the 250-year-old Charles City County Court House. Near here Chief Powhatan ruled over an extensive Indian confederation. You may remember that his daughter, Pocahontas, saved the life of Captain John Smith. The Indians called the river the Powhatan, but the early English settlers renamed it after their King, James I.

Less well known is that a free African-American community, one of the first in the Americas, flourished here in the 1600s, and that this is the birthplace of Lott Cary, the first African-American missionary to Africa and founder of Liberia.

Past Charles City, turn right on Virginia Highway 619 to visit Sherwood Forest Plantation, home of president John Tyler, and the last plantation on this drive. As previously mentioned, Tyler became president in 1841 when his neighbor William Henry Harrison died after 30 days in office. Tyler had a long history of political office, serving twice as governor of Virginia, and in both the U.S. Senate and U.S. House of Representatives.

The property is maintained by and still home to Tyler's grandson, Harrison Tyler. Because the home has remained in the family, most of the original furnishings and memorabilia have been preserved.

It may seem remarkable that the grandson of the man who was president in 1845 is still living. Grandfather-president John Tyler had two successive wives who bore him 15 children—the most offspring of any president. He was 63 when he fathered his youngest son, Lyon. Lyon, in turn, was 75 when he became the father of his youngest son and present owner, Harrison Tyler.

The main mansion was built in several pieces over 170 years beginning in 1660. Known as the longest frame dwelling in America, it reached its present length—more than 300 feet—when President Tyler added a 68-foot ballroom for dancing the Virginia Reel.

In addition to the main house and its elegant furnishings, many of the original outbuildings have been restored, including the tobacco barn, kitchen, laundry, smoke house, milk house, and law office. A formal garden makes up some of the 25 acres of terraced gardens, woods, and lawn.

Continue on VA 5. You leave Charles City County and its plantations as you cross the wide Chickahominy River on a drawbridge, with a good view of the James River on the right. Urban life—signs, malls, condos, and stores—soon appears. Continue straight at the light at Five Forks and follow VA 5 into Williamsburg and the end of the drive. Williamsburg is at the midpoint of the Colonial Parkway, Drive 15, and described in that selection.

15
Colonial Parkway
Jamestown to Williamsburg to Yorktown

General description: Colonial Parkway connects the two sections of Colonial National Historical Park: Jamestown, in 1609 the first English settlement in America; and Yorktown, a colonial town and scene of the last skirmish of the Revolutionary War. Between the two is Colonial Williamsburg, former colonial capital with more than 500 restored buildings. The parkway itself is a 23-mile, two-lane highway and can be easily driven in less than an hour; nearby are many historical and other attractions that may induce you to linger longer.

Special attractions: For many visitors, history, theme parks, and shopping malls are bigger draws here than the scenery, but don't miss the views of the shoreline, water, and woods along the parkway. Jamestown, Yorktown, and Colonial Williamsburg each played a unique role in the history of the United States.

Location: Colonial National Historical Park, off Interstate 64 by Williamsburg in the east-central part of the state.

Drive route numbers: Colonial Parkway, plus unnumbered loop tours at Yorktown and Jamestown.

Travel season: All year. Summer can be hot and muggy with large crowds.

Camping: None within the federal areas. Nearby are several privately owned campgrounds.

Services: Gas, motels, hotels, and restaurants of every kind and price range are available all year round in the surrounding area.

Nearby attractions: The entire area is a major tourist destination. There is plenty to do for every taste when you get tired of history. In addition to Jamestown, Yorktown, and Colonial Williamsburg, some of the more popular attractions include Carter Groves, Busch Gardens, Water Country USA, Anheuser-Busch Brewery Tour, and Williamsburg Pottery.

 The Drive

There's not much to this drive—23 miles of scenic parkway, plus 7 or 8 miles of optional loop tours at both ends. But these 23 miles span almost 400 years of American history, linking Jamestown, the first permanent, English-speaking settlement in North America in 1607 and first colonial capital, with Yorktown, an early colonial port town and site of the last battle of

Drive 15: Colonial Parkway
Jamestown to Williamsburg to Yorktown

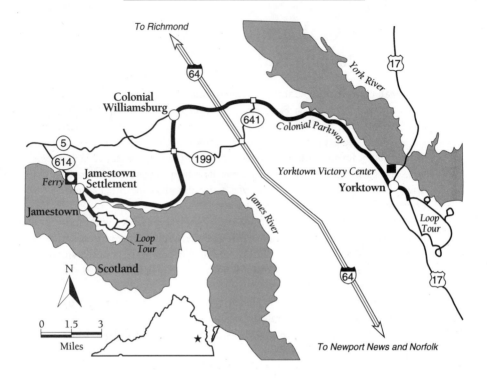

the Revolutionary War when the British army surrendered to General George Washington in 1781. Midway between the two is Colonial Williamsburg, the restored second capital of Virginia, with more than 500 buildings restored or renovated to look much as they did in the 1700s.

Jamestown, Yorktown, and the Colonial Parkway collectively make up Colonial National Historical Park. One fee admits you to all of these. State facilities—Jamestown Settlement and the Yorktown Victory Center—adjoin the federal areas and have separate fees. Although you can start at either end or at several places in the middle, including Williamsburg, it is chronologically correct to begin where it all began, at Jamestown, southwest of Williamsburg on an island in the James River.

Jamestown was colonized in 1607 by about 100 colonists who made the four-month trip from England in three small ships. Two years later there were some 500 settlers. It was a difficult and dangerous life in the wilderness; during the winter of 1609–1610, known as the "Starving Time," more than three-fourths of the colonists died.

In 1607 about 100 colonists established Jamestown near here on a small island in the wide James River.

Despite the many hardships of frontier life, the colonists persevered; the town grew, and became the first colonial capital. Today the town of Jamestown is gone, except for some foundations and ruins adjacent to the river.

An 8-mile loop road through the flat marshes of the island gives you an idea of what the original settlers faced, helped by markers and illustrations along the way. Several short trails lead off from the loop road to scenic views of the James River and tidal bays. You'll also see numerous wading and shore birds, and may sight distant ships down the river toward Newport News and Norfolk.

The visitor center gives the story of their struggle for survival, with numerous articles of daily colonial life on view. You can walk past many of the excavations and fragile foundations, and may be able to join a tour and see archeologists continuing their work. Recent discoveries have uncovered the foundations of James Fort, built in the 1620s and believed to have been eroded away by the James River. Nearby is the reconstructed Glasshouse, where craftspeople in period clothing demonstrate seventeenth-century glassblowing techniques.

Just outside the federal area is the Jamestown Settlement, maintained by the state of Virginia. No ghost town here: Full-size replicas of the three ships that carried the settlers over the Atlantic, the first fort, and an Indian village vividly bring colonial times to life. Costumed guides, with chickens underfoot, lend realism.

And just beyond the Jamestown Settlement are the slips for the Jamestown-Scotland Ferry. This free, modern ferry, maintained by the state of Virginia, plies its way between Jamestown and Scotland, Virginia, 24 hours a day. A trip over, even if you turn around and come right back, gives you a waterside perspective of Jamestown that is similar to what the original settlers saw as they made their way up the James.

When you're ready to leave Jamestown, head toward Williamsburg and Yorktown on the two-lane, limited-access parkway. For several miles you pass marshes and inlets along the James. Egrets and shore birds are common. Frequent turnoffs with roadside markers provide good viewpoints.

The road heads inland through stands of hardwoods, including oak and sycamore. The parkway was built in the 1930s. The route was chosen for its scenic beauty and has no historical significance. The maximum speed limit is 45. Be alert for the numerous bike riders who frequent the road.

The well-marked exit for Colonial Williamsburg is about 9 miles from Jamestown, just before a short tunnel that passes underneath the complex. Williamsburg became the second colonial capital when it was moved from Jamestown in 1699. The restoration of Colonial Williamsburg was created and funded by John D. Rockefeller, Jr. A variety of tours, demonstrations of colonial living and activities, and even libations and meals at colonial taverns provide rich insights into eighteenth-century life.

Underpasses and bridges on the Parkway show the design and brick facings that help maintain the colonial atmosphere and architecture of the area.

In addition to the complex of Colonial Williamsburg itself, you may want to visit nearby attractions included in admission, such as the Abby Aldrich Rockefeller Folk Art Center and formal gardens. One walking tour, "The Other Half," focuses on colonial life as experienced by slaves. In addition, there are many private homes and gardens that are open to the public. Adjacent to the historical district is the colonial-style campus of the College of William and Mary. Drive 14, The Plantation Road, concludes at Williamsburg.

The parkway continues past Williamsburg. The many bridges and other structures are detailed in brick to reflect the colonial architecture of the region. As the area grew, new intersections and crossings developed, and each one required a bridge. Modern developments, such as the I-64 underpass completed in 1965, continue to use the traditional brick facing and railing details over concrete arches as designed for the original spans.

You emerge from the woods on the shore of the York River at Felgrass Creek, a popular local picnic and fishing area. The river remains on your left as you drive the last few miles to Yorktown. The large structure extending several thousand feet into the river is a U.S. Navy munitions pier where arms are loaded onto naval ships.

The parkway ends at the Yorktown visitor center, which features a full-size mock-up of the gun deck and other sections of a British frigate that was sunk during the Battle of Yorktown. The federal area preserves two distinct sections in addition to the visitor center: the historic town of Yorktown, and the Battle of Yorktown. The battle in 1781 followed a three-week siege by General George Washington that surrounded the British army. The British had been held in place by an offshore French blockade. After a few minor skirmishes, the British, lead by Commander Lord Cornwallis, surrendered to Washington, effectively ending the Revolutionary War; however, a formal peace treaty was not signed for another two years.

Two 8-mile loop tours on wooded, winding roads cover the battle area. During the drive you can trace the battle and see siege lines (trenches), cannons, and other equipment, with intermittent views of the York River. The loop tours are the end of the drive.

Unlike Jamestown, a living town of Yorktown still exists. The park preserves much of the historical area, including some private, historic homes. From the visitor center a guided foot tour of Yorktown passes by the Yorktown Victory Monument erected by the United States at the centennial in 1881 to commemorate the French alliance during the war.

Just outside the federal area is the Yorktown Victory Center, maintained by the state of Virginia. The exhibits here feature the events leading to the Revolutionary War. Frequent reenactments of daily colonial life by costumed interpreters are held.

At the Yorktown Centennial in 1881, 100 years after the Battle of Yorktown, the United States erected the 95-foot-tall Yorktown Victory Monument to commemorate France's help during the war.

16

Over and Under Big Walker
Wytheville–Bluefield Loop

General description: This 75-mile loop drive through the mountains of southwest Virginia follows the old highway up, down, and around the mountains to West Virginia. From there, you reverse direction and return on a modern interstate, tunneling through the mountains you climbed over earlier. Most of the drive is through the Jefferson National Forest and incorporates the Big Walker Scenic Byway.

Special attractions: Jefferson National Forest, the Big Walker Scenic Byway and lookout, scenic mountain views, small country towns, and a restored Indian village. The contrast between the winding, hilly old roads and the modern interstate with tunnels adds to the interest.

Location: Southwest Virginia, outside of Wytheville near the intersection of Interstates 77 and 81.

Drive route numbers: U.S. Highway 52; Virginia Highway 717; Interstate 77. Forest Service Road 206 for the optional trip to the Big Bend Picnic Area and viewpoint.

Travel season: Both spring and fall give the mountain views special hues and colors. Winter travel can be hazardous, but the views of snow-covered mountains from the top of Big Walker are rewarding.

Camping: Camping is available at the Stony Fork campground in Jefferson National Forest near the beginning of the route. There are private campgrounds at the Wytheville KOA and at Fort Chiswell and Bluefield, Virginia.

Services: Gasoline, restaurants, motels, and hotels are available in Wytheville and Bluefield, West Virginia. Small towns along the route have gasoline and restaurants.

Nearby attractions: The Shot Tower Historical State Park in Austinville shows how rifle balls were made from chunks of lead. The New River Trail State Park, headquartered in Austinville, provides more than 57 miles of hiking along a former railroad bed stretching from Fries to Pulaski. Bluefield, West Virginia, is the terminal for Coal Heritage Trail, a West Virginia scenic drive.

 The Drive

This 75-mile loop drive is a study in contrasts. Beginning near Wytheville, the trip out follows VA 717 and US 52, the old, two-lane, winding and hilly

Drive 16: Over and Under Big Walker
Wytheville–Bluefield Loop

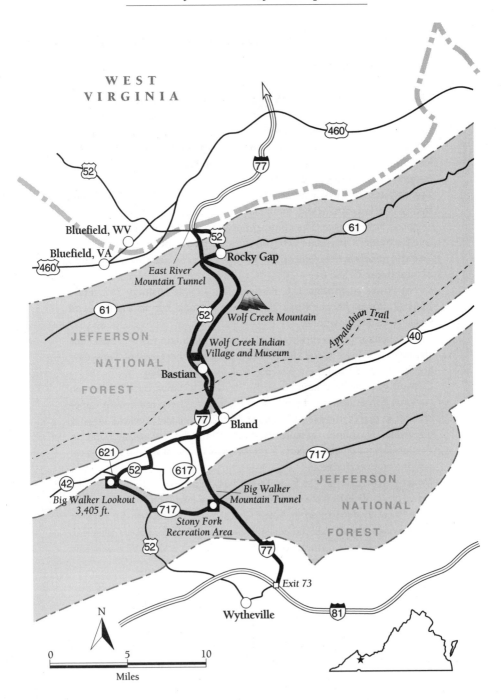

road over Big Walker Mountain, past several small towns, and across other ridges to the West Virginia border. From there you reverse direction and take modern I-77 to cruise leisurely through the rugged country on gentle curves, tunneling under Big Walker Mountain to your starting point. The trip out on old roads takes several hours. The return trip on the interstate takes about 25 minutes. Most of the drive is within Jefferson National Forest.

The craggy hills and mountains of the Valley and Ridge province in southwest Virginia presented a formidable barrier to travel to early settlers. There is little level land; early roads followed old trails across the numerous, unbroken ridges and wound around countless mountains and smaller hills. As automobile travel developed, the highways followed the old trails, and US 52 (formerly known as US 21) between Wytheville and Bluefield, West Virginia, is no exception. Today US 52 still climbs up, over, and down Big Walker Mountain and then follows numerous curves and crosses smaller hills and valleys.

Four-lane I-77 considerably shortened this trip, and made it easier and faster. Cliffs were blasted away to eliminate curves, and cut-and-fill smoothed out many small grades. Two mile-long tunnels eliminated the long and difficult mountain drives over Big Walker and East River Mountains.

Wytheville, just south of the drive, is known for its numerous antique shops and outlets, many of which reflect its German, Scotch, and Irish heritage. Lead mines near Austinville south of the city were important during the Revolutionary War and during the Civil War, when the mines became a major source of lead for the Confederacy. The metal was taken to the nearby Shot Tower (now a state historical park) where the lead was heated, then dropped in water to make rifle balls and other shot.

To begin the drive, take Exit 47 of I-77 at the intersection with VA 717, about 5 miles north of Wytheville. This is within the Jefferson National Forest. Ahead on I-77 are the long ridge of Big Walker Mountain and the twin portals of the Big Walker Mountain Tunnel.

Go west on two-lane VA 717 which parallels the ridge, following the signs for the Big Walker Mountain Scenic Byway. In a few miles you pass the entrance to the Stony Fork Recreation Area, which has a campground, hiking trails, and fishing in Stony Fork Creek.

At the intersection with US 52, turn right. The road soon heads uphill for the long climb up Big Walker Mountain. At the top, elevation 3,405 feet, is the privately owned Big Walker Lookout which features a 100-foot fire tower, gift shop, and restaurant. The most outstanding views are from the top of the tower above the treetops, but you can enjoy excellent views from the gift shop without making that long climb. In one direction lie ridges, valleys, farmlands, and small towns; in the other is an unspoiled sea of mountain peaks and forests.

Twin tunnels bore through Big Walker Mountain, 2,500 feet below the lookout tower.

When Big Walker Lookout opened in 1947, it was advertised as "The highest point on US 21 between the Great Lakes and Florida." U.S. Highway 21 no longer exists, but the lookout is still far higher than any place in the Great Lakes or Florida. The facility is open from April through October. A fee is charged to climb the tower.

The lookout also marks the place where Confederate heroine Mary Tynes crossed the mountain in 1863 to warn the residents of Wytheville of a raid by Union Colonel John Toland. Alerted by the alarm, the fighting townspeople turned away the raiders, killing Toland during the skirmish.

A side trip from the lookout on Forest Service Road 206 leads 4 miles to the Big Bend Picnic area. This tree-shaded site, at an elevation of 4,000 feet, has excellent views of the Valley and Ridge province.

After a short ride along the ridge, it's a curvy downhill trip off Big Walker. You emerge in an open valley. At the intersection with Virginia Highway 42, turn right, continuing on US 52 along one of the few level stretches on this section of the drive.

In a few minutes you cross I-77, marking the end of the Big Walker Mountain Scenic Byway. Just beyond is the town of Bland, county seat of Bland County, with an imposing courthouse. U.S. Highway 52 turns left in Bland.

It's all uphill and downhill from here. If you look carefully you may spot markers for the Appalachian Trail as it crosses the highway a few miles past Bland. On the far side of the small town of Bastian is the Wolf Creek Indian Village and Museum, where interpreters wear native costumes. Carbon dating has shown that the site was occupied as early as 1215 A.D.

For a few miles, U.S. 52 parallels I-77 where it cuts through Wolf Creek Mountain. (Before the interstate was built, the old road went up and over this mountain.) The cliffs and half-mile-long outcrop on the other side of the interstate are composed of Clinch sandstone of Silurian age.

A steep climb after the town of Rocky Gap brings you to the foot of East River Mountain to an intersection where US 52 joins I-77. Ahead are the twin tunnels that bore through the mountain. You can't drive on the old road over this mountain; it was eliminated when the interstate was built, and the only way across is through the tunnel.

So follow US 52/I-77 through the mile-long modern tunnel. About half-way through, watch for the boundary marker as you pass into West Virginia several hundred feet underground. Take the first exit after the tunnel (in West Virginia), still following US 52, which turns left at the stop sign.

This marks the end of the "old road-US 52" portion of the drive. For a respite, you can follow US 52 a few miles into the town of Bluefield, West Virginia, adjacent to its smaller sister city of Bluefield, Virginia. The Coal Heritage Trail, a West Virginia scenic drive, begins near Bluefield.

If you want to return immediately, turn left (south) on US 52/I-77 and drive through the East River Mountain Tunnel again. At the other end, stay on I-77. There are sweeping views ahead of the steep hills you recently drove through.

I-77 cuts though the hills with gentle, high-speed curves. It's a fast trip, mostly downhill. In a few minutes you pass the cliff and outcrop where US 52 parallels the highway. A few miles later, to the left of the highway, is a large, operating coal mine. The tall structure is the shaft building on top of the lift (elevator) used to haul men and coal from the mine.

The drive flattens out for a few miles as you approach the ridge of Big Walker Mountain and the drive through the tunnel, several thousand feet below the road you traversed earlier. On the other side is Exit 47 for VA 717 where you began the drive at the scenic byway. You can exit here, or stay on I-77 another 7 miles to Wytheville and the intersection with I-81.

17

Buchanan to Blacksburg
Mountain Streams and Valley

General description: This 70-mile drive, almost entirely within Jefferson National Forest, follows twisty Craig Creek surrounded by peaks of the Allegheny Mountains. It then climbs into the mountains and traverses an unspoiled farming valley virtually all the way to the end of the drive at Blacksburg.

Special attractions: Unspoiled, clear mountain streams, scenic mountain vistas, curvy roads, and very few towns. This drive appeals to those who want a mountain drive with no tourist distractions or towns. Most of the drive is along a designated Virginia Scenic Byway.

Location: Western Virginia, off Interstate 81 at Buchanan between Lexington and Roanoke.

Drive route numbers: Virginia Highways 43, 615, and 42; U.S. Highways 220 and 460.

Travel season: Spring, summer, and fall are the preferred seasons. Heavy mountain snows may temporarily close the road in winter. Exercise caution because much of the drive is through isolated country.

Camping: A private campground with about 100 sites is located at Natural Bridge, 10 miles north of Buchanan.

Services: Gasoline, restaurants, and motels are available in Buchanan at the beginning of the drive and along US 460 at the conclusion. New Castle, near the middle of the drive, has gasoline. Make sure you have sufficient gas.

Nearby attractions: Natural Bridge, a 215-foot limestone arch, is about 10 miles north of Buchanan on I-81, and can easily be combined with this drive. Once owned by Thomas Jefferson, it was known as one of the Seven Wonders of the World. The Peaks of Otter on the northern section of the Blue Ridge Parkway, Drive 6, are south of Buchanan. Mountain Lake resort lies north of Newport.

 The Drive

This 70-mile drive leaves from the town of Buchanan. The narrow, two-lane road follows the Upper James River and one of its twisting tributaries upstream between the peaks of the Blue Ridge Mountains. Then, in a dramatic change of pace, the drive climbs over the ridgeline and passes through a small valley between the ridges. The drive concludes in a short

Drive 17: Buchanan to Blacksburg
Mountain Streams and Valley

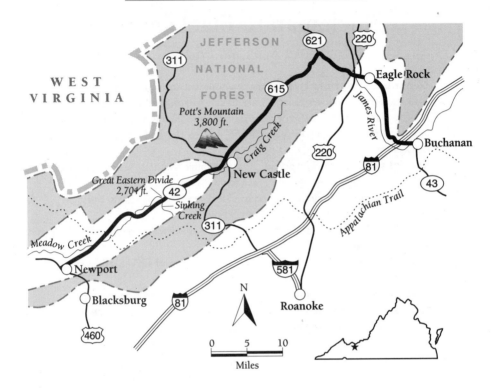

stretch of four-lane highway ending in the city of Blacksburg, home of Virginia Tech (Virginia Polytechnic Institute, or VPI).

Buchanan is off Exit 167 of I-81, about midway between Roanoke and Lexington and about 10 miles south of the exit for Natural Bridge. You can also reach Buchanan from the northern section of the Blue Ridge Parkway, Drive 6, by taking VA 43 north just past the Peaks of Otter.

In the 1850s Buchanan was an important commercial town at the western terminus of the James River and Kanawha Canal, which ran from Richmond to Buchanan. Several piers and remnants of the canal can be seen north of town along the river. The town, including much of Main Street, was flooded in 1985 and recovery has been slow. Today Buchanan's main industries are beef and dairy cattle, timber, and limestone and crushed stone; tourism is increasing in importance.

From downtown Buchanan, go north on VA 43, a Virginia Scenic Byway. Note the swinging pedestrian bridge, the only footbridge in Virginia to

The clear waters of Craig Creek make it popular with trout anglers.

cross the James River. After you cross I-81, look back at the town and the gap for the James River. The drive enters the Jefferson National Forest.

The road, known locally as Narrow Passage Road, follows the curves of the James River. This section of the James, many miles upstream from the head of navigation at Richmond, is known to anglers for its sometimes elusive smallmouth bass and muskie.

You drive through a narrow pass at Eagle Rock where sandstone outcrops stand almost vertical. Just beyond, the road curves around Rathole Mountain on the right to the stop sign at US 220 where VA 43 ends.

Make a sharp left turn onto US 220, crossing the James River. Go about 2 miles and turn right on VA 615. (Note: A new bridge over the James is planned that will let you go directly from VA 43 to VA 615, eliminating the present stretch on US 220.)

The drive now follows Craig Creek, a much smaller stream than the James. In a few miles, at the intersection with VA 621, go left, still following VA 615. The creek, with its sinuous S-curves, clear water, rocky bottom, and tree-shaded shoreline is popular with trout anglers. Although the stream may (or may not) be shallow enough to wade across at the time of your visit, houses built on stilts attest to frequent floods and high water.

The road follows the creek, but is noticeably less curvy. Occasional stretches lead away from the creek to higher ground through thick woods. A few trailheads lead into the adjacent national forest and high country to the right. Gradually you emerge into more open country, with views of the Allegheny Mountains. The prominent peak ahead is Pott's Mountain, elevation 3,800 feet.

Virginia Highway 615 ends at New Castle, the county seat of Craig County. Go left one block and turn left on Main Street. At the stop sign cross VA 311 and go straight on VA 42.

The drive immediately begins a steep and curving climb up from the valley floor. In about a mile is an overlook on the left where you can gaze down on New Castle 1,000 feet below, and at the numerous peaks surrounding the town. After further climbing, the drive enters a broad highland valley about a mile wide between mountain ridges.

Eight miles from New Castle you cross the almost imperceptible Great Eastern Divide at an elevation of 2,704 feet. Behind you the waters flow into Craig Creek, then east into the James River, Chesapeake Bay, and the Atlantic Ocean. Ahead, on the other side of the divide, water flows into Sinking Creek, then west into the New River, the Kanawha, and Ohio, to join the mighty Mississippi, where it then flows south to the Gulf of Mexico and eventually into the Atlantic. Look for a highway marker delineating the spot.

There is little level ground in this high country. The open fields, too steep in most places for crops, support numerous herds of grazing cattle and sheep. You pass trim and prosperous-looking farmhouses, barns, and silos, many with small gardens wherever a plot of level ground can be found. Many fields also contains grazing teams of Percheron and Clydesdale horses. These big workhorses are used on slopes that are too steep on which to safely use tractors.

The valley flattens out, virtually surrounded by mountain peaks, as the drive follows Sinking Creek. In a few miles you pass the little town of Sinking Spring. As you may guess, the name "Sinking" means that you are in limestone cave country where many of the small streams disappear underground, often emerging several miles farther downstream.

Beyond Sinking Spring, the Appalachian Trail crosses the drive. A few miles beyond there, VA 43 ends at the intersection with US 460. Off the drive and a few miles to the right on US 460 is the road to the resort area at Mountain Lake. At 4,000 feet elevation, Mountain Lake is the highest lake in the state.

The drive turns left on US 460 for a speedy, downhill trip with several panoramic views ahead to Blacksburg and the end of the drive.

Blacksburg is home to Virginia Polytechnic Institute and State College, more commonly known as Virginia Tech. Also in Blacksburg is Smithfield Plantation, an eighteenth-century mansion restored to its colonial grandeur and open to the public during the warmer months.

The gap shows where the James River flows through the Blue Ridge Mountains on its way to Richmond and the Atlantic.

18

Burke's Garden
Valley in the Sky

General description: Burke's Garden is a 10-mile-long valley entirely surrounded by mountains. The valley consists of fertile, rolling farmland, pastures, and woods. This unstructured 40-mile drive allows you to explore this unique area. You can also visit the Historic Crab Orchard Museum and Pioneer Park which has exhibits ranging from a 500-million-year-old fossil tree to an original 1831 McCormick reaper.

Special attractions: Burke's Garden itself is the main attraction, including the enclosed valley, rich farmlands, woods, and mountains views.

Location: Southwest Virginia, near Tazewell. Tazewell is on Virginia Highway 16 about 25 miles north of Marion.

Drive route numbers: Virginia Highways 61, 623, 666, 625, 667, and 627.

Travel season: In winter, the altitude and bowl-like shape of the valley bring heavy snows which can temporarily close roads. Otherwise the trip can be made at any time. As in most of Virginia, each season has its own special beauty. Autumn is especially beautiful, when the altitude and local climate combine to turn the leaves exquisite shades of yellow, orange, and red. The Burke's Garden Fall Festival, held the last Saturday in September, is timed to coincide with the peak leaf season; it is also the heaviest travel day of the year.

Services: All services are available in Tazewell. Limited food and gasoline can be obtained in the valley.

Camping: Not available.

Nearby attractions: The Pocahontas Exhibition Mine northeast of Tazewell provides guided tours through an exhibition coal mine.

 # The Drive

Burke's Garden east of Tazewell is an elliptical valley about 10 miles long, totally enclosed by circular Garden Mountain. Inside this sparsely populated valley is some of the richest farmland in the state with views in all directions of rolling country with mountains in the background. This short drive, less than 40 miles long and with no specific route to follow within the valley, will allow you to explore the nooks and crannies of this unique area.

Before visiting Burke's Garden you may want to spend some time in the Historic Crab Orchard Museum and Pioneer Park west of Tazewell on

Drive 18: Burke's Garden
Valley in the Sky

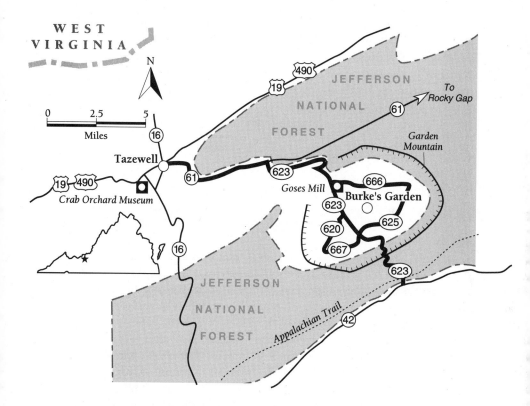

U.S. Highway 19. Among the historical exhibits (and history as defined by Crab Orchard begins more than half a billion years ago) are mammoth bones and teeth, another fossil—a Lepidodendron tree that grew during the coal-forming eras—and a replica of a Native American village, surrounded by a wooden stockade.

More recent exhibits include early automobiles and one of Cyrus McCormick's original 1831 reapers. A dozen buildings and associated exhibits depict life in the Virginia mountains in the 1830s. The facility is open all year, but with reduced hours in winter.

To begin the drive go east from Tazewell on VA 61. This is a two-lane road through mostly open farming and cattle country. In a few miles a low range of hills, about 600 feet higher than the valley, appears on the left. This is the southern rim of circular Garden Mountain; inside Garden Mountain lies Burke's Garden.

Turn right on VA 623, about 8 miles from Tazewell. In a few minutes the narrow road begins the long and curvy climb to the top of the ridge. As you ascend, views of the valley behind you appear through the trees, and you see outcrops of sandstone as you approach the ridgeline.

As you come over the ridge, the elliptical bowl of Burke's Garden lies before you. A short, downhill run brings you to the floor of the valley.

The valley was discovered in 1748 by James Burke. According to legend, Burke, who was part of a survey crew, buried some potato peelings by a campfire. The peelings took root and provided a welcome crop of potatoes for next year's survey party, who laughingly referred to "Burke's garden." The name for the valley stuck, and the mountain that encircles the valley is now known as Garden Mountain. But Burke never got to enjoy his namesake valley. Legend says that he moved to North Carolina and was a neighbor to Daniel Boone.

At an elevation of about 3,100 feet, the valley has the reputation for being the highest, coldest, greenest, and prettiest valley in the state. Some or all of this may be true, but it is a fact that the rich limestone soils combine with other factors to make this rolling valley floor one of the most fertile farm areas in the state.

For a complete tour of the valley, sometimes known as "God's Thumbprint," turn left on VA 666 by the bridge at Goses Mill, and follow the complete loop around the valley. The route numbers will change as you drive around, but that will not be a problem. All roads will take you back to VA 623, the main road down the middle of the valley.

Along the way you'll pass farms with herds of beef and dairy cattle, fields of corn and other crops, small streams, and groves of hardwoods. Several stands of maple line the road, magnificent in autumn with their orange and red attire. There are several home-based quilt and craft shops, some run by Amish settlers. And visible in all directions is the encircling ridge of Garden Mountain rising from the valley floor. What you won't see are many people. About 600 folk—far less than the number of cattle—live within the valley's 20,000 acres.

Many people think that Burke's Garden is a crater that formed from some ancient, cataclysmic volcanic eruption. Actually the valley and enclosing mountains are the results of erosion of folded sedimentary rocks. In Ordovician time, 500 million years ago, reefs deposited limestone and dolomite in warm ocean waters. These rocks were then covered by sandstone. Later, when the Appalachian Mountains were formed, the rocks that now make up Burke's Garden were uplifted and folded into a dome or plunging anticline.

Millions of years of erosion slowly wore away the uplifted sandstone rocks in the middle of the dome. Today the valley floor is underlain by the dolomite and limestone, and the harder and more resistant sandstone makes up the ring of encircling mountains.

Limestone boulders border a small creek near the center of the valley in Burke's Garden.

The "town" of Burke's Garden consists of a general store and post office in the middle of the valley along VA 623. The Central Church is the oldest Lutheran place of worship in the state; the adjacent cemetery has hand-carved German headstones dating back to the 1700s. The nearby former school-house is now the town meeting hall. (School children go by bus over the mountain to Tazewell.)

The valley is lovely at any time of the year. Changing leaf colors, high-lighted by the brilliant red maples, peak in late September. The Burke's Garden Fall Festival is held the last Saturday of that month with numerous craft exhibits and sales of local produce. The festival is also the heaviest travel day of the year, and about the only time when you will see more than a few cars along the valley roads. Heavy snow can temporarily close roads in winter; more than 100 inches of snow have been recorded some years.

When you're ready to leave, go north on VA 623 (the way you came in) over Garden Mountain to VA 61 and turn left to return to Tazewell.

An alternative exit is to go south on VA 623 at the other end of the valley. This is an unpaved, narrow, curvy road with steep grades for 10 miles through a portion of Jefferson National Forest. You will see dirt roads, hardwood forests, laurel, dogwood, Virginia creeper, and rhododendron but no facilities or houses. It is not recommended for trailers or those unsure of their mountain driving skills. It connects with Virginia Highway 42 between Bland and Virginia Highway 16.

19

Breaks Interstate Park

Virginia's Grand Canyon

General description: This is a 60-mile, pristine drive through woods and mountains with few towns or distractions along the way, giving a taste of rural Virginia as much of the state must have looked years ago. The drive ends at Breaks Interstate Park on the rim of the 1,600-foot deep canyon of the Russell Fork River, the deepest canyon in the eastern United States.

Special attractions: The unspoiled nature of the drive is perhaps its biggest attraction. At the end of the drive on the Virginia-Kentucky border lies the Breaks Interstate Park, known for its canyon of sheer walls and many recreational activities, including whitewater rafting, hiking, fishing, and horseback riding. Nearby is the John Flannagan Dam in Jefferson National Forest.

Location: Southwest Virginia, off Interstate 81 Exit 24. This exit is about 7 miles northeast of Abingdon, and about 20 miles southwest of Marion on I-81.

Drive route numbers: Virginia Highway 80.

Travel season: The drive can be made at any time of year, but most facilities at Breaks Interstate Park are closed from late October to April. Weekends in October attract large numbers of whitewater rafters when water is released from the James Flannagan reservoir.

Camping: The campground at Breaks Interstate Park has about 120 campsites, most equipped with all facilities. Several camping areas are scattered around the Flannagan reservoir area in the Jefferson National Forest.

Services: Gasoline and limited services are available in the small towns along the route. The Breaks Interstate Park has gasoline, a restaurant, and a lodge open from April to December.

Nearby attractions: The John Flannagan Dam and Reservoir in Jefferson National Forest provides numerous recreational activities. Abingdon at the start of the drive has many attractions and is described in Drive 20.

 The Drive

Don't take this drive if you want to visit museums, Civil War or other historical areas, large cities, or tourist attractions. The drive follows a two-lane paved, but sometimes rough, road uphill and down, mostly through the unspoiled beauty of Jefferson National Forest. It ends about 55 miles later at the cliffs and slopes of Breaks Interstate Park, the largest river canyon east of the Mississippi. Along the way you'll pass a few small towns, including Honaker, known as the Redbud Capital of the World. But most of the drive passes by woods, streams, and mountains, giving a view of rural Virginia as much of it looked 50 or 75 years ago.

Because of numerous steep grades and sharp curves, the first part of the drive (south of U.S. Highway 19) is not recommended for trailers more than 30 feet long.

The drive starts at VA 80 off Exit 24 of I-81. This is about 6 miles northeast of Abingdon via either I-81 or U.S. Highway 11. Abingdon is the starting point for Drive 20; its several attractions, including the famous Barter Theater, are described in that section.

Go north on VA 80, a two-lane, winding, and hilly road that passes through alternating forests and small farms. This section of the drive crosses the Valley and Ridge province of folded rocks made up of sandstone ridges and limestone valleys.

After several miles you cross in short succession the Holston River and the smaller West Fork of the Wolf River. The drive enters a spur of the Jefferson National Forest, and in a series of steep slopes and near hair-pin turns, climbs and descends several ridges. The forested slopes have restricted views because they are covered with both hardwood and pines, with thick groves of redbud, rhododendron, and other flowering shrubs.

You leave the national forest and descend into a broad, limestone valley. At the stop sign in Elk Garden at the intersection with four-lane U.S. Highway 19, turn right, still following VA 80. In 2 miles at Rosedale, turn left, still on VA 80; US 19 continues straight ahead.

Although still two lanes, VA 80 is wider here, and with fewer grades. The drive crosses the Clinch River and passes through the town of Honaker, which holds a Redbud Festival in April when the blossoms are at their peak.

Honaker also marks the sometimes indistinct boundary between the Valley and Ridge province of folded sedimentary rocks which you have been crossing, and the Appalachian Plateau to the north, of similar, but flat-lying rocks. The Appalachian Plateau in Virginia also includes numerous coal beds; coal mining is a major industry here, although you won't see much evidence of it on this drive.

You soon start to follow the Russell Fork River, which forms a narrow canyon barely wide enough for the road and the river in most places. Small towns such as Council are spread out along the road, one block wide and several blocks long. At Haysi, the high school is perched on a cliff and you'll see the stairs and overpass that students must use to cross the road.

In Haysi, Virginia Highway 63 leads left from VA 80 to the John W. Flannagan Dam and Reservoir in Jefferson National Forest. The rock and

Drive 19: Breaks Interstate Park
Virginia's Grand Canyon

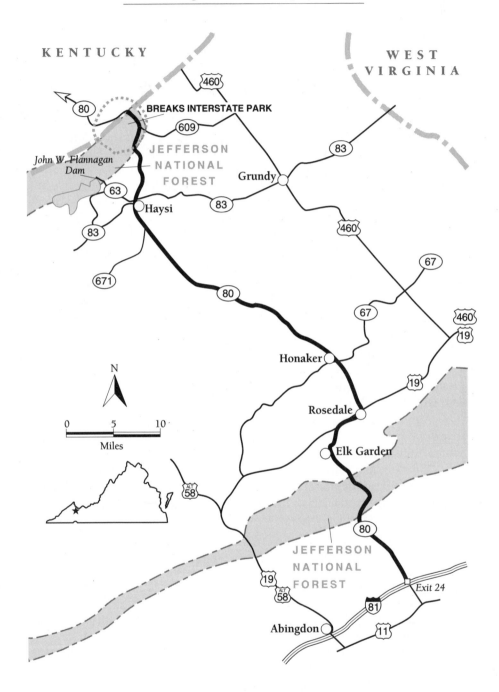

earthen dam, 250 feet high and 916 feet long, was completed in 1964 for flood protection. The reservoir is known for its walleye and bass fishing and also provides boating, swimming, hiking, hunting, and picnicking. It is the water supply for several local communities.

Water released from the dam flows down the Russell Fork River and through the canyon in the Breaks Interstate Park just ahead. The river flows north to join the Big Sandy River, which empties into the Ohio River.

Whitewater enthusiasts will instantly recognize the Russell Fork, renowned for its Class VI rapids. The best rafting occurs when water behind the dam is released downstream. Releases from the dam depend on water levels and supply, but major releases are usually scheduled for weekends in October, drawing hundreds of rafters.

Stay on VA 80. In a few miles you pass an overlook, giving you the first glimpse of the breaks; just beyond is the entrance to the park, where the drive ends. The main attraction of the park is the 1,600-foot-deep canyon that curves along the Russell Fork River for 5 miles. A paved road along the edge of the canyon leads to several overlooks, giving you numerous views of the canyon, river, tiny-looking railroad at the bottom, and distant, rolling mountains.

Reputedly, the breaks was visited by Daniel Boone in 1767. But it took until 1951 before a paved road was built through the area, linking Virginia and Kentucky; this permitted development of Breaks Interstate Park with portions in both states. The only other interstate park is Palisades State Park along the New York–New Jersey border on the Hudson River.

The park is sometimes called (with only a slight stretch of the imagination) the "Grand Canyon of the South" and less reverently as the "Grand Canyon with clothes on," in reference to the thick forest and underbrush that cover all but the steepest slopes. It's called "the breaks" because the Russell Fork gorge breaks up the long ridge of Pine Mountain.

The canyon is formed in limestone capped with red, mottled sandstone. The most impressive overlooks give you a view of the Towers, an almost isolated pyramid of rock surrounded by a 270-degree bend in the Russell Fork River. The gorge also contains an active rail line; you may see long trains loaded with West Virginia coal slowly grind through the canyon and several tunnels on their way to the Newport News seaport.

The region was logged clear in the late 1800s and early 1900s. Today mixed hardwood and pine cover most of the area, with thick growths of rhododendron, dogwood, and other wildflowers and shrubs.

There are several miles of hiking trails, including some leading to the floor of the canyon and to overlooks not accessible by car. The visitor center contains exhibits on the natural history and human history of the area; you can learn the true-life story about the Hatfields (in Virginia) and the McCoys (in Kentucky) whose long-lasting feud resulted in more than 65 murders.

The road and the river head into Kentucky at the edge of the Breaks Interstate Park.

A motor lodge, restaurant, and campground are open from April through October. Swimming (in a pool), boating and fishing (in a small lake) and horseback riding are available. Although the Russell Fork has some expert rapids, it has numerous tamer stretches, and you don't have to be an expert rafter to enjoy the sport. Novices are welcomed by several rafting companies that offer a variety of river trips from gentle to wild during the October rafting season. Check at the visitor center for more information.

When you leave the park, turn right (south) on VA 80 to retrace your route. Turn left (north) on VA 80, which descends to the valley floor and follows the Russell Fork into Kentucky on Kentucky Highway 80 to the intersection with U.S. Highway 460.

20

Abingdon–Big Stone Gap Loop
Coal Country and the Powell Valley

General description: Starting in southwest Virginia in Abingdon, site of the Barter Theater, the 75-mile drive heads into the Blue Ridge highlands. The drive combines visits to Virginia's coal country and Big Stone Gap, including several exhibits and museums, with the outstanding mountain scenery of the Powell Valley and the High Knob Recreation Area in Jefferson National Forest.

Special attractions: Abingdon and the Barter Theater, coal country, Big Stone Gap, the Coal Museum, the John Fox, Jr. Museum, the Powell Valley, Jefferson National Forest, and High Knob Recreation Area and observation tower.

Location: Southwest Virginia. The drive begins at Abingdon, off Exit 17, Interstate 81.

Drive route numbers: U.S. Highways 23, Business 23, and Alternate 58; Virginia Highway 619.

Travel season: Summer is the height of the travel season, when all attractions are open. Except for the side trip to High Knob, which may be closed because of snow in winter, most of the ride can be taken any time of the year.

Camping: Available in the High Knob Recreation Area near Norton in Jefferson National Forest.

Services: Gasoline, restaurants, and lodging are plentiful in Abingdon, Norton, Big Stone Gap and nearby Wise, and in most of the towns along the route.

Nearby attractions: The Guest River Gorge, the Virginia Creeper Trail (Drive 21), and the town of Bristol (starting point for Drive 22).

The Drive

Southwest Virginia is a land of contrasts, an up-and-down country of rugged, forested mountains and valleys, open, scenic vistas, and winding roads. The area is a mixture of prosperity and poverty, unspoiled natural beauty and coal mine slag heaps, thriving towns and struggling villages.

This 75-mile drive takes you through the heart of this country, from upbeat Abingdon through Norton and Big Stone Gap. Along the way you'll take a loop through coal mining country, pass through the sweeping grandeur of Powell Valley, and drive to the top of High Knob in Jefferson National Forest for a 360-degree view from the lookout tower. The drive ends at Norton.

Although you can complete the drive in one day, there is so much to see and do that two or three days is recommended. This will allow you time to enjoy some of the many attractions, such as a show at the Barter Theater, a visit to the Coal Museum, an outdoor performance of "The Trail of the Lonesome Pine," or to just savor the scenery of Powell Valley and the Jefferson National Forest.

The drive begins in Abingdon off Exit 17 of I-81. But spend some time in town before you leave. Abingdon is the oldest incorporated town west of the Blue Ridge. It is also the home to the world-famous Barter Theater.

The Barter Theater was opened in the Depression year 1933 by Robert Porterfield to help unemployed performers. Cash was scarce, so local residents often paid the actors with 40 cents' worth of chickens, eggs, ham, or vegetables. Reputedly, playwright George Bernard Shaw's royalty was paid in spinach; Tennessee Williams received a Virginia ham.

Today the Barter Theater is the state theater of Virginia, and pigs are no longer accepted in payment. The theater still presents comedy, drama, music, and mystery performances from March through December.

Steep hills and grades require numerous railroad trestles and bridges to haul coal from the mountains.

Drive 20: Abingdon–Big Stone Gap Loop
Coal Country and the Powell Valley

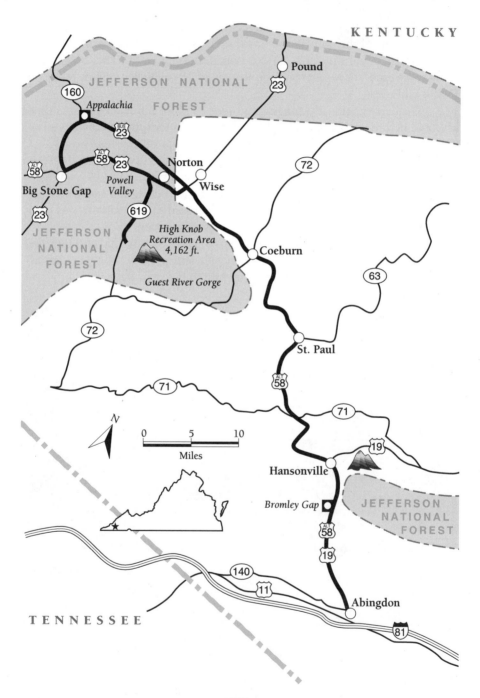

Across Main Street from the Barter Theater is the venerable Martha Washington Inn. Built in 1832 as a palatial home for a retired general, this stately institution has also served as a college for young women and a Civil War hospital. The original living room is now the inn's main lobby.

Abingdon is also the northern trailhead for the Virginia Creeper Trail, a 34-mile foot and bicycle trail through the rugged Mount Rogers National Recreation Area to the North Carolina border. The trail follows an old railroad bed and uses several trestles that have been adapted for footpath use; Drive 21, Mount Rogers Loop, parallels the Virginia Creeper Trail for several miles.

This drive leaves Abingdon heading west and north on four-lane US Alternate 58/19 past rolling fields and farmland typical of the Valley and Ridge province and the Shenandoah Valley in northern Virginia. After crossing the North Fork of the Holston River, the drive passes through Bromley Gap in Clinch Mountain. The road cuts are mostly in folded sandstone.

As you approach Hansonville, 2,600-foot-high Hansonville Peak is visible on your right. At Hansonville, turn left on US Alternate 58; US 19 goes right. The drive continues through open valleys, farmland, and rounded hills.

Soon you come down a steep hill and cross the Clinch River at the bypass around St. Paul. This town marks the approximate boundary between the Valley and Ridge geologic province that you have been driving through and the Appalachian Highlands to the west.

The road alternates between tree-covered, steep-sided, narrow valleys and more open farmland, following the bends in the Guest River. Nearby in Jefferson National Forest is the Guest River Gorge Trail. The trail, which is under development, follows a former railroad bed past canyons and cliffs for 5.5 miles. The trailhead is reached by taking Virginia Highway 72 south from Coeburn.

Although the drive is not as spectacular as the trail, in several narrow places there is barely room for the highway and river. You pass some small coal mines; many more of these marginal operations are no longer producing. A railroad roughly parallels the road through the nearby hills, but is rarely visible except for several railroad trestles that span the creek valleys off the main drive.

Look for a 5-foot-wide, circular blue pipe that bridges the highway. This is a coal transporter, part of a complex of conveyer belts that moves the coal from several mines to the rail siding below. If you look carefully to the right, you can see the transporter rising steeply to a coal mine high in the hills.

You come over the hill outside Norton for an open view of the small valley and town. The loop portion of the drive to Big Stone Gap and back begins here at the four-way intersection with US Alternate 58, US 23, and US Business 23. The outbound section of the loop follows an older, narrow two-lane road along a stream valley through coal country to Big Stone Gap; the return portion is via US 23/Alternate 58, a modern, four-lane highway through the scenic Powell Valley, with a side trip to High Knob.

To the left of the intersection are small cliffs with the tree-covered hills of Jefferson National Forest behind them. Bordering the cliffs and forest you will see a new highway that looks interesting and inviting, and it is: This will be the return route for this loop.

Go straight (south) on US Business 23 through the main street of Norton. (The route numbers may be poorly marked. Do not take US 23 or US 23/Alternate 58.) As you pass through town, notice that even the bank names—Lonesome Pine Black Diamond Bank, the Miners Exchange, and others—let you know you are in coal country.

US Business 23 soon leaves Norton on a narrow, winding, two-lane road with barely room for the highway, the Powell River, and the railroad between cliffs and hills on either side. This is the heart of coal country. You pass several small mines and railroad coal loading sidings. Coal seams are visible in many roadcuts, as are the remaining high walls of old strip mines.

Now closed, this coal transporter processed 4 to 5 million tons of coal a year, loading it directly into railroad cars.

This stretch gives you a good idea of what much of this area looked like before modern roads.

At Appalachia you pass the closed Westmoreland Coal Company Bullit Mine Complex. Bituminous coal from several nearby mines was moved by conveyer belts, many still visible through the trees, to the facility where it was temporarily stored in the huge silo-like buildings. Coal from more distant mines was transported here by truck. The coal was then loaded onto trains of 100 cars or more. In its heyday the complex processed 4 to 5 million tons of bituminous coal a year. In the early 1900s large mining companies controlled all the mines; with company-owned stores, housing, and even medical clinics, they controlled much of the miners' lives, too.

Even though the big mines have been mostly played out and closed, this is still a major bituminous coal mining center. What remains—smaller deposits, thinner coal seams—are now being worked by individuals or small companies. Today some 300 mines still operate in Virginia's southwest corner, supplying about 14 million tons of coal annually and employing more than 4,000 miners. Although travel and tourism have increased markedly to provide many jobs, full employment is still an unreached goal.

From Appalachia to Big Stone Gap is a bucolic, 5-mile drive along the Powell River. The gap itself, just outside town, is a breach in resistant sandstone where the Powell River has cut through Big Stone Mountain.

The town of Big Stone Gap is the setting for local author John Fox, Jr.'s best-selling novel, "The Trail of the Lonesome Pine," published in the late 1890s. The book, which takes place during the boom years of the coal industry, describes the love of a local girl for a mining engineer. The novel was the first million-dollar best-seller and has been made into a movie at least three times. A drama created from the book is held in an outside theater in Big Stone Gap several times a week during the summer months. The author's home is now the John Fox, Jr. Museum, and contains authentic family furnishings and memorabilia. If that isn't enough, there is another museum, the June Tolliver House, named after the book's heroine.

The Southwest Virginia Museum has numerous exhibits on frontier life of early pioneers in the area. The Coal Museum, owned by the Westmoreland Coal Company, has a variety of mining exhibits, artifacts, and photographs, many procured from local mines and miners' homes.

If some places in Big Stone Gap look familiar, it may be because you saw the movie "Coal Miner's Daughter." Many of the scenes were filmed here. Also nearby, but you won't see it, is Virginia's new maximum-security prison for problem inmates. This is one of several prisons recently built in southwest Virginia. The prisons have aroused some controversy among local residents, but they do provide much-needed employment opportunities for many former miners.

The observation tower at High Knob, 4,162 feet high, gives a 360-degree view.

When you're ready to leave Big Stone Gap, follow US Business 23 to US 23/Alternate 58. Go north (toward Norton and Wise). In a few moments you will be climbing up the broad, open Powell Valley. The four-lane highway hugs the left side of the valley, at times supported over the valley by cantilevers. At the head of the valley an overlook gives sweeping views of farms and houses 1,000 feet below, framed by distant mountains. It is hard to believe that this pastoral scene is only a few miles from the heart of coal country.

As you approach Norton again, you'll have good views of the town to your left. On the right are alternating cliffs and forest marking the boundary of Jefferson National Forest. Take the exit at VA 619 and turn right toward the forest and the High Knob Recreation Area.

This two-lane road twists, turns, and climbs steadily uphill to the observation tower atop High Knob, elevation 4,162 feet. The tower is a 30-second walk from the parking area, and gives you the best view in the state of Virginia for the least effort. On clear days you can see five states from this 360-degree panorama.

Camping, picnicking, and swimming in a 5-acre lake are other popular activities in the recreation area. On your way down the mountain, look for the turn to Flag Rock, which overlooks Norton. The Stars and Stripes were first flown here in the early 1900s by an immigrant who, happy to be in his new country, put up the flag pole; the present flag is maintained by the town.

Return to US 23/Alternate 58 and turn right. In another mile you will be at the four-way intersection of US Alternate 58, US 23, and US Business 23 and the end of the drive. From here you can return to Abingdon via US Alternate 58, or stop at the nearby towns of Norton and Wise.

Old Glory has been waving from Flag Rock overlooking Norton since the early 1900s.

21

Mount Rogers Loop
Virginia's Subalpine High Country

General description: This mountain drive encircles Mount Rogers (elevation 5,729 feet) and Whitetop Mountain (elevation 5,570 feet), Virginia's highest peaks. It passes from lush, wooded mountain streams along the Virginia Creeper Trail into the subalpine high country in Jefferson National Forest. Most of this 60-mile drive is within the Mount Rogers National Recreation Area, known for its hiking, camping, fishing, and scenic beauty. The drive encompasses the Mount Rogers Scenic Byway. Several side trips, such as the gravel summit road of Whitetop Mountain, take you into the heart of the high country. Most of the drive is over paved, but very curvy, two-lane roads with some steep grades. There are numerous campgrounds.

Special attractions: The Virginia Creeper Trail, a loop through the subalpine high country around the two tallest mountains in Virginia, the open meadows of Grayson Highlands State Park, a drive to the top of Whitetop Mountain, outstanding views, mountain trout streams, hiking, fishing, camping, biking, and skiing.

Location: Southwest Virginia, south of Marion and east of Abingdon along the North Carolina border.

Drive route numbers: U.S. Highway 58; Virginia Highways 16 and 603. Side trips appear on Virginia Highways 600 and 89 for Whitetop Mountain summit, and on unnumbered roads to Grayson State Park.

Travel season: All year, but use caution in winter when heavy mountain snow can close roads temporarily.

Camping: The Forest Service maintains six campgrounds; two are open year-round. Horse stables and camping are available at the Forest Service's Fairwood Livery and Horse Camp. Camping and horse stables are also maintained at Grayson Highlands State Park.

Services: Motels, restaurants, and gasoline are accessible in Damascus and nearby Abingdon and Marion. Food and gasoline can be obtained at the intersection of VA 603 and VA 600.

Nearby attractions: Abingdon and the Barter Theater are about 10 miles west of Damascus. Abingdon is the starting point for Drive 20. Hungry Mother State Park is north of Marion, about 15 miles from Troutdale.

Drive 21: Mount Rogers Loop
Virginia's Subalpine High Country

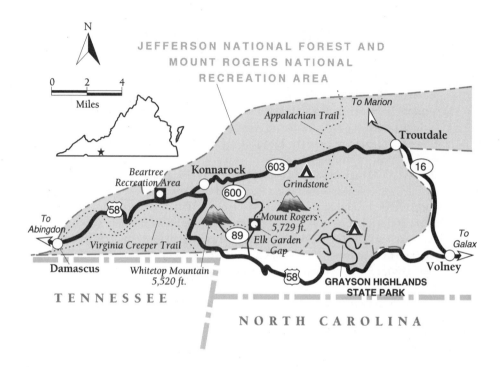

 The Drive

The 115,000-acre Mount Rogers National Recreation Area in Jefferson National Forest surrounds some of Virginia's finest mountain scenery, including Mount Rogers and Whitetop Mountain, the state's two highest peaks. Most of the drive is within the Mount Rogers National Recreation Area, which itself is part of the Jefferson National Forest.

The National Recreation Area was established in 1966, partly to offset population pressures on Great Smoky Mountain and Shenandoah National Parks. Today it contains several hundred miles of hiking, skiing and horse trails, numerous campgrounds, lush woods, and streams. The drive makes a 360-degree circuit around the high country with several side trips to subalpine areas.

The drive begins in Damascus on US 58 about 10 miles east of Exit 9 on Interstate 81 at Abingdon; Abingdon is also the starting point for Drive

20 to Big Stone Gap. This drive follows US 58 east from Damascus, paralleling the Virginia Creeper National Recreation Trail to Volney. From Volney, the drive makes a complete circuit around the two highest peaks in the state: Mount Rogers (elevation 5,729 feet) and Whitetop Mountain (5,570 feet), following VA 16 and VA 603, and rejoining US 58 past the small town of Konnarock.

Two side trips lead you through the heart of the high country. The first visits Grayson Highlands State Park, known for its views, hiking, camping, fishing, and other outdoor activities; the second leads you along the uppermost highway in Virginia on a dirt Forest Service road to the summit of Whitetop Mountain.

The drive totals about 80 miles, including the side trips, but your total mileage will be more because you will have to retrace part of the drive. You can make the trip in one day, but if you want to do any hiking, biking, horseback riding, or just take a leisurely sightseeing trip, two or more days are recommended.

The portion of the drive along US 58 from Damascus to Volney, along with the portion along VA 603 from Troutdale to Konnarock, comprises the 55-mile Mount Rogers Scenic Byway, a nationally designated scenic drive.

A variety of campsites, with facilities that range from the primitive (pit toilets, no drinking water) to upscale (warm showers, hot and cold running water) are available. Reservations are accepted for some campgrounds; others are on a first-come basis. Check with the Forest Service or Grayson Highlands State Park for current information. Motels are available in nearby Abingdon and Marion.

You can also start at Troutdale at the intersection of VA 16 and VA 603 by joining the drive and heading west on VA 603. A complete circuit from here will require retracing part of your route. Troutdale is about 15 miles south of Exit 45 on I-81 at Marion via VA 16. This drive itself is quite scenic and passes through several miles of Jefferson National Forest. Another possibility is to start at Abingdon and follow US 58 to Damascus to join the drive. You can also start at either Abingdon or Marion and end at the other city. This elongated drive will be 120 to 130 miles long, depending on which part of the route you retrace.

The main drive starts in Damascus. The Appalachian Trail runs down the main street (US 58) of this small mountain town, making it a popular rest stop and resupply area for hikers. Follow US 58 east out of town and into the woods along a narrow, winding stream valley. An understory of rhododendron, spectacular when in spring bloom, covers both sides of the road in many places. (Note: Because of the many sharp curves, the Virginia Department of Transportation does not recommended pulling trailers more than 35 feet long on this section.)

Hikers return from an ascent of Mount Rogers at Elk Garden Gap.

The road parallels the Virginia Creeper Trail for several miles, with several points of access. The trail, which runs 34 miles from Abingdon to the Virginia-North Carolina border, follows an old logging railroad bed, which in turn follows the trace of a Native American footpath. It is known for its 32 converted railroad trestles that cross the numerous gorges, and gentle railroad-category grades, making it attractive for hiking, biking, horseback riding, cross-country skiing, and even wheelchair traveling. The streams, stocked with trout, attract fishermen. Look for a view of one of the trestles near a turnoff with picnic tables.

The trail reputedly received its name from the heavily loaded logging trains which crept up the grades, but some say it was named for the Virginia Creeper plant, which is commonly found here, along with rhododendron. If you plan to be dropped off for a one-way hiking or biking trip, be forewarned that the trail is constantly downhill from Abingdon to North Carolina, and uphill in the other direction.

In about 4 miles you pass Beartree Recreation Area, which features camping, picnicking, a large lake for fishing, and a sandy beach for swimming. At the intersection with VA 603, bear right on US 58. You will end up here at the completion of the main loop of the drive.

The drive soon begins to climb. The woods thin out as you cross Whitetop Gap and come into open fields, leaving the national forest. You may think you are in the land of Christmas trees, which are grown here in profusion. To the left is Whitetop Mountain; in the distance to the right, waves of mountains stretch to the horizon in North Carolina.

The drive passes the intersection with VA 600, the other end of the side trip to Whitetop Mountain. About 4 miles after this intersection, you pass the historic Mount Rogers Combined School, one of the few schools that still teaches kindergarten through high school in the same building, and is still in use after almost a century of service.

About 3.5 miles beyond that, at 3,698 feet in elevation, is the entrance to Grayson Highlands State Park on the southeast flank of Mount Rogers. The park's roads wind through the alpine high country with its northern hardwood and evergreen forest, open grassy meadows (called "balds"), and outstanding mountain views.

The park's many trailheads provide jumping-off places for numerous hikes, including the summit of Mount Rogers. Horseback riding along the Virginia Highlands Horse Trail is popular. You can rent horses or bring your own; Grayson Highlands is the only Virginia state park that provides stables. Other activities include camping, picnicking, fishing, and hunting (licenses required), and special cultural events. The park is open all year and, averaging more than 100 inches of snow annually, is popular with winter campers and cross-country skiers.

The visitor center, at almost 5,000 feet, has excellent exhibits of area rocks and mountain crafts, from quilts and musical instruments to children's toys. In the warmer months the Rooftop of Virginia Crafts Shop operates a small store in the visitor center.

When you leave Grayson Highlands State Park, drive down the twisty entrance road back to US 58 and turn left. At Volney, about 7.5 miles from the state park at the intersection of US 58 and VA 16, turn left (north) on VA 16. This section of road is outside the National Recreation Area and national forest and skirts the eastern flank of the loop. You pass many small farms and herds of grazing cattle with occasional views of the high country to the left.

Virginia Highway 16 leads in 7 miles to Troutdale, a former logging town, at the intersection of VA 16 and VA 603. When logging was at its peak, around 1900, the town had a population of more than 3,000; today's population is about 200.

Nearby is the former home and burial site of author Sherwood Anderson, who lived here from 1925 until his death in 1941. Anderson is known as one of the founders of the American School of Realism which strongly influenced Ernest Hemingway and William Faulkner. Anderson was also the publisher of two local weekly papers.

Turn left on VA 603 to traverse the northern section of the loop. You soon enter thick woods of the national forest, parallel to Fox Creek. In about 2 miles you pass several cascades along Fox Creek, a popular area with trout anglers. Just past this you will see fences along the stream bank that are part of the Fox Creek Riparian Area Recovery Project. The fences are designed to keep livestock away from the stream bank, so as to reestablish vegetation and prevent erosion. Increased vegetation will also provide shade, lowering the temperature of the stream water and benefiting trout (and presumably trout anglers).

You pass by open pastures, often occupied by grazing cattle and horses, and the entrance to the Fairwood Livery and Horse Camp. This campground for people and horses has sites, visible from the road, equipped with hitching posts and feedbag holders, and with room to park horse trailers. It should be obvious that horseback riding is a popular activity; the national recreation area has several hundred miles of trail through both woods and high country. If you didn't bring your own horse, you can rent one here and arrange for a variety of self-guided or guided trail rides.

Just past the horse camp, the drive crosses the Appalachian Trail. This spot is a well-known drop-off and pick-up point for hikers; on summer weekends there may be several cars parked nearby.

Soon you pass the turnoff for the Grindstone Campground. Its numerous campsites, hot showers, and 400-seat outdoor amphitheater make it a favorite for family camping and another jumping-off spot for hikers.

Past the campsite on the left are several views of Mount Rogers with its bare ridges and spruce- and fir-covered top. Because it is not a prominent peak, it was not recognized as the highest point in the state until accurate surveys in the early 1900s. None of the mountain peaks are high enough to extend above a true timber line, but many of them have treeless summits or bare, open meadows and ridges. These balds, as the bare spots are known, probably resulted from forest fires.

A few stores and gas stations mark most of the town of Konnarock. The town is spread out along US 58 between the intersections of VA 603 and VA 600. Like other towns along the drive, Konnarock reached its peak population when lumbering was an important industry. When it was a lumber-mill town, around 1900, several thousand people lived here; today there are about 100 residents.

The main loop continues straight ahead on VA 603 through the rest of Konnarock for about a mile to the intersection with US 58 and the end of the drive; but many people will turn left on VA 600 for the side trip to the high county and Whitetop Mountain.

Virginia Highway 600 is a paved, two-lane road that soon begins to zig and zag as it climbs. In about 3.5 miles you come to the broad, open meadows of Elk Garden Gap. Several trails lead to the summit of Mount Rogers, including the Appalachian Trail, which crosses the road, and the Virginia Highlands Horse Trail, often used as a winter ski trail. The Appalachian Trail here is the shortest—4.5 miles—but one of the steepest trails to the summit. Mount Rogers itself, Virginia's highest at 5,729 feet, lies to the left as a humpbacked ridge. Although the summit is tree covered, many of the ridges and slopes leading to the top are bare, affording excellent views.

The mountain is named for William B. Rogers, Virginia's first state geologist and a founder of the Massachusetts Institute of Technology. The geology of Mount Rogers itself raises some puzzling questions for geologists. They agree that the rocks that make up the mountain are volcanic in origin—primarily metamorphosed basalts and rhyolites of late Precambrian age. But they seem to be unrelated to rocks of similar age elsewhere in Virginia and North Carolina, so earth scientists are unsure how they fit into the overall geologic framework of Virginia.

Continue about a mile on VA 600 to the left turn on VA 89, which leads in several miles to Whitetop Mountain, Virginia's second highest at 5,570 feet. The road is not suitable for recreational vehicles or trailers. Be very careful on this road during cloudy and inclement weather, and remember that the weather can deteriorate in a few minutes in the high country. Fog—low lying clouds here—and thunderstorms are both common year-round.

Virginia Highway 89 is a narrow, winding gravel road with several steep grades, and is the highest automobile road in the state. The last mile

Near the summit of Mount Rogers are thin stands of red spruce and other trees. Mount Rogers and Whitetop Mountain are the only places in Virginia where the red spruce is found.

consists of switchbacks through open country to a viewpoint just below the summit with good views of Mount Rogers. On clear days you see ridge after ridge stretching to the horizon into North Carolina.

The woods behind the parking area are predominantly red spruce; this tree is found in Virginia only near the summits of Whitetop and Mount Rogers. Unfortunately you can't visit Whitetop's actual summit, which is fenced in and covered with a forest of antennas and communication towers.

Turn around and carefully drive back down the switchbacks. Notice the red and white "barber pole" markers that help keep you on the road during foggy weather.

Retrace VA 89 to the junction with VA 600. What you do next depends in part on where you began the drive. Turn right on VA 600 and go 2 miles to the intersection with US 58. At US 58, you can turn right to Damascus or left to Volney and VA 16. Or, you can turn left on VA 600 and retrace the drive to VA 603 at Konnarock where you turn left to Damascus (and then to Abingdon) or right to Troutdale (and then to Marion).

22

Cumberland Gap
On the Trail of Daniel Boone

General description: This 100-mile drive follows the Wilderness Trail hacked out by Daniel Boone in 1775 through southwest Virginia to the narrow mountain pass at Cumberland Gap where Virginia, Tennessee, and Kentucky converge. Most of the drive is through small, mostly unspoiled towns. The drive concludes at the 2,440-high Pinnacle Overlook in Cumberland Gap National Historical Park where you can gaze down at the gap and the long range of mountains extending to North Carolina. The drive features a stop at Natural Tunnel State Park where you can ride a chair lift down to the huge cave entrance.

Special attractions: Cumberland Gap National Historical Park, Natural Tunnel State Park, Wilderness Road.

Location: Southwest Virginia and adjacent portions of Kentucky and Tennessee.

Drive route numbers: U.S. Highways 58 and 25E; Virginia Highways 690 and 871; Pinnacle Road.

Travel season: All year long. Some facilities may be closed during the colder months. Occasional snow may make travel difficult.

Camping: Camping is permitted year-round in Cumberland Gap National Historical Park; the campground in Natural Tunnel State Park closes in winter.

Services: All services are available in Bristol, Virginia; Bristol, Tennessee; Middlesboro, Kentucky; and many of the smaller towns.

Nearby attractions: Jefferson National Forest, Abingdon and the Barter Theater, and Big Stone Gap. See Drive 20 for descriptions of this area.

 The Drive

Cumberland Gap is a narrow mountain pass through the Appalachian Mountains in southwest Virginia near the Tennessee-Kentucky border. From time immemorial the gap has been used as a gateway through the mountains to the west. It is a record of civilization moving west and the passing of the western frontier. It was first used by migrating herds of buffalo and deer, later by American Indians, fur traders, hunters, and pioneers, and today by cars and trucks.

Drive 22: Cumberland Gap
On the Trail of Daniel Boone

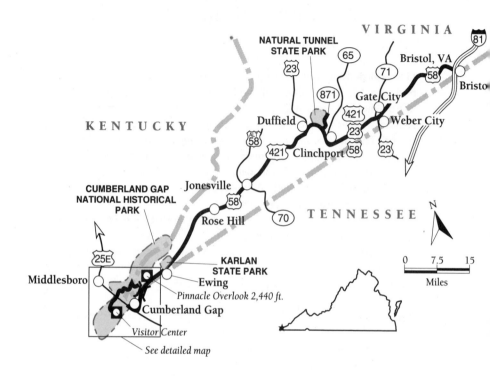

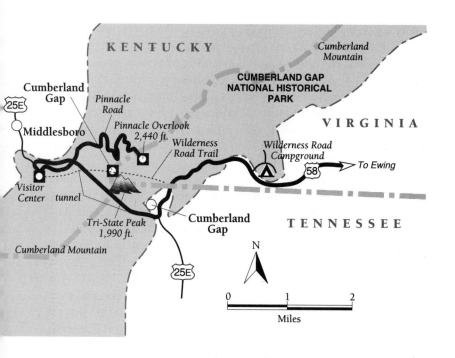

KENTUCKY

Cumberland
Mountain

CUMBERLAND GAP
NATIONAL HISTORICAL
PARK

VIRGINIA

Cumberland
Gap

Pinnacle
Road

25E

Middlesboro

Pinnacle Overlook
2,440 ft.

Wilderness
Road Trail

Wilderness Road
Campground

To Ewing

58

Visitor
Center   tunnel

Tri-State Peak
1,990 ft.

Cumberland
Gap

TENNESSEE

Cumberland Mountain

N

25E

0   1   2

Miles

Native Americans learned of the gap by following the buffalo, and it soon became a major route for hunting parties. It was also used by rival raiding parties and was known as the Warrior's Path.

The gap was rediscovered by European Thomas Walker in 1750. But the French and Indian Wars intervened and prevented additional exploration. It wasn't until 1775 that Daniel Boone, with 30 axmen, marked the Wilderness Trail from eastern cities through Cumberland Gap to the Kentucky frontier. Settlers followed, and by 1792 the population of Kentucky was more than 100,000, and the territory was admitted to the Union.

By 1800 some 300,000 settlers had followed Boone's winding trail through Cumberland Gap on their way to the Kentucky River and the present cities of Lexington and Louisville. It was not a one-way trail: the pioneers were often met by fur traders, hunters, and farmers driving livestock heading east to the seaboard cities.

This drive follows about 100 miles of US 58, the Wilderness Trail, traversing in a few hours what took the western settlers months to cross. Much of the drive is over a two-lane road along Cumberland Mountain past small towns, fields of corn and tobacco, tobacco barns, and grazing cattle. Along the way you'll pass Natural Tunnel State Park. Natural Tunnel is a ten-story-high, 850-foot-long cave; a chair lift or short hike can take you down to the creek and railroad that pass through the tunnel.

The drive ends at Cumberland Gap National Historical Park, just over the state line in Middlesboro, Kentucky. The old road that formerly wound through the Gap has been replaced by a four-lane tunnel that bores beneath Cumberland Mountain. From the park you can drive back into Virginia to 2,440-foot-high Pinnacle Overlook for a magnificent view of the gap and the surrounding states, or hike to the gap which is being restored to look like the wagon trail it once was.

The drive begins at Exit 1 of Interstate 81 in southern Virginia, just over the Tennessee border and outside the city of Bristol. There are two Bristols: State Street straddles the line between Bristol, Virginia, and Bristol, Tennessee.

From the interstate, drive west on U.S. Highway 58/421. Almost immediately you are driving through low, rolling, mostly bare hills on a winding, two-lane road past farmhouses and barns. Cattle graze on the slopes, and crops of corn and tobacco are grown on the small patches of level ground.

Some of the occasional road cuts are covered by kudzu, a broadleaved, invasive vine. Although kudzu is a relatively minor detraction here, in many parts of Virginia and the south the vine grows so prolificly that it crowds out and kills virtually all other growth.

The drive crosses the North Fork of the Holston River and intersects U.S. Highway 23 at Weber City, about 26 miles from Bristol. Bear right on

The railroad tracks disappear into the darkness of Natural Tunnel.

US 58/421/23, a four-lane highway. To the right you look over Gate City. There is a distinct, wooded ridge on the left. After you follow the ridge for several miles, the road curves uphill to the right into steep and hilly, wooded country.

Thirteen miles from Weber City, turn right onto VA 871 at the sign for Natural Tunnel State Park. Natural Tunnel, the stellar attraction of the park, is an 850-foot-long cave that is open at both ends. The cave entrance is as high as a ten-story building. A natural stream, Stock Creek, and a man-made railroad, the Southern Railroad, both run through the cave.

As you approach the park, you will see a 200-foot-high cliff of reddish gray limestone appear ahead. The cliff is a remnant of a collapsed or eroded cave that was once part of a larger Natural Tunnel cave system.

Continue on VA 871 to the park visitor center about a mile from US 58. Natural Tunnel may have been visited by Daniel Boone during his quest for the Wilderness Road, but the tunnel was not widely known until 1832 when Colonel Stephen Long explored and publicized it. It soon became a major tourist attraction, and was immensely popular in the late 1800s. William Jennings Bryan called it "The Eighth Wonder of the World."

Because the tunnel provides an easy grade through this hilly country, railroad tracks were laid through it in 1890. It is still used today by several coal and freight trains of the Southern Railroad. The tunnel has been a state park since 1967.

Like most limestone caves, Natural Tunnel was created from the slow solution of acidic groundwater on the limestone rock. Stock Creek did not form the cave, but was diverted into it after the cave had begun forming. The creek did help to enlarge the cave and shape the spacious walls and roof.

The fastest and easiest way to visit the tunnel entrance is to take the 500-foot-long chair lift to the bottom of the gorge. The chair lift, which is wheelchair accessible, runs daily in summer and on weekends spring and fall. The rail line through the tunnel is still used several times weekly by coal trains; if your timing is fortuitous, you may see one. You can't enter the tunnel itself, but park authorities provide occasional guided caving trips through the tunnel.

The visitor center contains exhibits on the geology and history of the area, including a display of various narrow-gauge railroad tracks. Several hiking trails lead to scenic overlooks or to the tunnel. There is a swimming pool, picnic area, and about 20 camp sites. Moderate fees, which may be seasonal, are charged for the chair lift and for some services.

When you leave the park, follow VA 871 back to US 58/421/23 and turn right. About 5 miles from the park, just before Duffield, go left on two-lane US 58/421. US 23 turns right, leading to Big Stone Gap and Drive 20.

Past Duffield, US 58 heads west, past small towns and farms through a broad, open valley. Parallel to the road on the right is Powell Mountain and, farther on, Cumberland Mountain, the unbroken ridge that was such a barrier to western exploration. You are following the Wilderness Road.

At Jonesville, US Alternate 58 heads northeast to Pennington Gap and then to Big Stone Gap. Jonesville is the birthplace of Dr. Alexander T. Still, who headed west to found the first school of osteopathy in 1892 in Kirksville, Missouri.

Cumberland Mountain, actually a long ridge, looms larger and larger on the right with prominent white cliffs of sandstone near the crest. The cliffs were a well-known beacon to the early pioneers, a sign that they were making progress on their western trek, and perhaps giving them the inspiration and hope to continue. At the slow pace of a wagon train or on foot, the cliffs were visible for several days.

Some 20 miles of US 58 along this stretch are being rebuilt as a four-lane highway. The goal is to relocate the highway away from the original Wilderness Road, and develop and maintain the Wilderness Road itself as a hiking and footpath corridor. The new four-lane highway, while scenic, will bypass some of the picturesque smaller towns and villages, such as Rose Hill and Ewing. In many places you can leave the four-lane highway and drive on the parallel older road through these and other small towns.

Cumberland Gap National Historical Park straddles Cumberland Mountain north of US 58 from the town of Ewing to the gap itself. Several side roads to the right lead to trailheads and are jumping-off places for wilderness camping.

A few miles past Ewing, VA 690 leads right to Karlan State Park. This park, which is under development, preserves some of the original wagon tracks in the Wilderness Trail and the Robert Ely mansion built in the 1870s to service trail travelers. Check locally to see what facilities are available.

In a few more miles, US 58 enters the boundaries of Cumberland Gap National Historical Park. The road begins a gradual climb up the side of Poor Valley Ridge. A well-marked road to the right leads to the main campground and some trailheads for the park.

If you have driven through Cumberland Gap prior to 1997, the next stretch of road may confuse you. Before 1997, US 58 led directly through the gap to US 25E and park headquarters in Middlesboro, Kentucky. Today the road through the gap is closed, and you reach park headquarters in Kentucky, and Pinnacle Gap in Virginia, by passing through a slice of Tennessee and a tunnel under Cumberland Mountain. Follow US 58 to its end outside the town of Cumberland Gap, Tennessee, at the state line at the junction with four-lane US 25E in Tennessee.

Go north (to your right) on US 25E, following the signs to the park and Middlesboro, Kentucky. You soon enter one of the twin 4,600-foot tunnels, speeding under Cumberland Gap in a way never dreamed of by Daniel Boone or the 200,000 settlers who followed. You cross into Kentucky midway through the tunnel. The entrance to Cumberland Gap National Historical Park is about a half-mile past the tunnel portal, before reaching the town of Middlesboro.

Turn into the park. The Pinnacle Road, which leads to the Pinnacle Overlook in Virginia and the end of the drive, is the first left-hand turn as you enter the park. But your first stop should be the visitor center for orientation.

Cumberland Gap National Historical Park was established by Congress in 1940 to preserve the history of westward migration, including the Wilderness Road and Cumberland Gap. World War II and lack of funding delayed opening of the park until 1955. The park today encompasses about 20,000 acres in Kentucky, Virginia, and a small part of Tennessee. Most of the park is a semi-wilderness extending for 20 miles along the ridge of Cumberland Mountain, a portion of the boundary between Virginia and Kentucky.

In addition to the gap and the visitor center, the park includes some 50 miles of hiking trails (including the popular Ridge Trail), a 160-site campground, picnic areas, several wilderness campsites, and the Hensley Settlement, a restored farm community that can be reached by trail or park shuttle. The park also includes Cudjo Cave which is closed for several years for

From the Pinnacle Overlook, a string of small lakes and mountain peaks stretches into Kentucky to the horizon.

renovations and primitive trail restoration. The visitor center has exhibits and a small museum. Guided hikes and other interpretive programs are scheduled during the warmer months.

The development plan for the park includes restoring the trail through the gap to as historically correct and natural a state as possible. This has led to the closing of US 58 through the gap and the building of the twin tunnels underneath Cumberland Mountain. Access to the gap itself, which will be restored to look like a 1790 wagon trail, will be by short foot trails from both the Kentucky and Virginia sides. Making US 58 in Virginia a four-lane highway is also part of this overall development plan. Details and updates on the progress of this restoration are available at the visitor center.

The Pinnacle Road is a narrow, winding, two-lane road that crosses back into Virginia and climbs to the 2,440-foot-high Pinnacle Overlook. The road has several hairpin curves and is closed to trailers and vehicles more than 20 feet long. A short trail leads from the parking area to several scenic vistas.

The view from the overlook shows Cumberland Gap 1,000 feet below, and the otherwise unbroken sweep of the mountain barrier that has had such a profound influence on American history. Signs and maps point out other features, including the twin tunnels and Tri-State Peak where Virginia, Kentucky, and Tennessee meet. On very clear days it is possible to see the Great Smoky Mountains in North Carolina.

The drive ends at the Pinnacle Overlook. However, you must turn around and negotiate the hairpin turns back to the visitor center. When you leave the park, turn right (east) on US 25E to return to Virginia and US 58, or turn left (west) on US 25E to go to Middlesboro, Kentucky.

The twin roadways of U.S. Highway 25E tunnel under Tri-State Peak, just out of sight to the right, where Virginia, Kentucky, and Tennessee meet.

Appendix: Sources of More Information

For more information on lands and events, please contact the following agencies and organizations.

Drive 1: Shenandoah Valley Loop

Civil War Information Center
Kurtz Building, 2 N. Cameron Street
Winchester, VA 22601
540-722-6367

George Washington National Forest
Forest Supervisor
P.O. Box 233
Harrison Plaza
Harrisonburg, VA 24401
540-885-8028

New Market Battlefield State Historical
  Park
Box 1864
New Market, VA 23844
540-740-3101

Drive 2: Leesburg Loop

Loudoun County Visitors Center
108-D South Street SE
Leesburg, VA 22075
800-752-6118

**Drive 3: George Washington Memorial
  Parkway**

Arlington National Cemetery
Arlington, VA 22200
703-607-8052

Mount Vernon Ladies' Association
Mount Vernon, VA 22121
703-780-2000

Drive 4: Piedmont–Blue Ridge Vistas

Barboursville Vineyards and Ruins
Route 777, Box 136
Barboursville, VA 22923
540-832-3824

Gray Ghost Vineyards
14706 Lee Highway
Amissville, VA 22002
540-937-4869

Warrenton-Fauquier County Visitors
  Center
183A Keith Street
Warrenton, VA 20186
540-347-4414

Drive 5: Skyline Drive

Potomac Appalachian Trail Club
118 Park Street SE
Vienna, VA 22180
703-242-0315
(For information on backcountry hiking
  and camping)

Shenandoah National Park
3655 U.S. Highway 211E
Luray, VA 22835-9036
540-999-3500

Drive 6: Blue Ridge Parkway North

P. Buckley Moss Museum
150 P. Buckley Moss Drive
Waynesboro, VA 22980
540-949-6473

Blue Ridge National Parkway
400 BB&T Building
One Pack Square
Ashville, NC 28801
828-298-0398
800-842-9163

Peaks of Otter Lodge
P.O. Box 489
Bedford, VA 24523
540-586-1081

Drive 7: Blue Ridge Parkway South

Blue Ridge National Parkway
400 BB&T Building
One Pack Square
Ashville, NC 28801
828-298-0398
800-842-9163

Drive 8: Fredericksburg and Spotsylvania
    Battlefields

Fredericksburg and Spotsylvania National
    Military Park
120 Chatham Lane
Fredericksburg, VA 22404
540-786-2880

Spotsylvania County Visitors Center
4704 Southpoint Parkway
Fredericksburg, VA 22407
800-654-4118

Drive 9: Northern Neck

Caledon Natural Area
11617 Caledon Road
King George, VA 22485
540-663-3861

George Washington Birthplace National
    Monument
R.R. 1, Box 717
Washington's Birthplace, VA 22443
804-224-1732

Reedville Fishermen's Museum
504 Main Street
Reedville, VA 22539
804-453-6529

Stratford Hall Plantation
Stratford, VA 22558
804-493-8038

Westmoreland State Park
Montross, VA 23219
804-493-8821

Drive 10: Eastern Shore

Chincoteague National Wildlife Refuge
P.O. Box 62
Chincoteague, VA 23336-0062
757-336-6122

Drive 11: Chesapeake Bay Bridge-Tunnel

Chesapeake Bay Bridge and Tunnel
    District
32386 Lankford Highway
P.O. Box 111
Cape Charles, VA 23310-0111
757-331-2960

Drive 12: Goshen Pass and Lake Moomaw

Lexington Visitor Center
106 E. Washington Street
Lexington, VA 24450
540-463-3777

Virginia Horse Center
Lexington, VA 24450
540-463-2194

Drive 13: Lee's Retreat

Appomattox Court House National
    Historical Park
P.O. Box 218
Appomattox, VA 24522
804-352-8987

Virginia's Retreat
P.O. Box 2107
Petersburg, VA 23804
800-6-RETREAT

Virginia Civil War Trails
550 East Marshall Street
Richmond, VA 23219
888-CIVIL WAR
(For other Civil War Trails)

Drive 14: The Plantation Road

Berkeley Plantation
Charles City, VA 23030
804-829-6018

Evelynton Plantation
Charles City, VA 23030
800-473-5075

Richmond National Battlefield Park
3215 E. Broad Street
Richmond, VA
804-226-1981

Sherwood Forest Plantation
Charles City, VA 23030
804-829-5377

Shirley Plantation
Charles City, VA 23030
800-232-1613

Drive 15: Colonial Parkway

Colonial National Historic Park
Box 210
Yorktown, VA 23690
757-898-3400

Colonial Williamsburg Foundation
Box 1776
Williamsburg, VA 23187
800-447-8697

Drive 16: Over and Under Big Walker

Big Walker Lookout
US 52 North
Wytheville, VA 24382
540-228-4401

Wolf Creek Indian Village
Route 1, Box 1530
Bastian, VA 24314
540-688-3438

Drive 17: Buchanan to Blacksburg

Forest Supervisor
Jefferson National Forest
5162 Valleypointe Parkway
Roanoke, VA 24019
540-265-5100

Drive 18: Burke's Garden

Burke's Garden
P.O. Box 462
Burke's Garden, VA 24608
540-472-2114

Historic Crab Orchard Museum and
    Pioneer Park
Route 1, Box 194
Tazewell, VA 24651
540-988-6755

Drive 19: Breaks Interstate Park

Breaks Interstate Park
P.O. Box 100
Breaks, VA 24607
540-865-4413

Dickenson County
    Chamber of Commerce
P.O. Box 1068
Clintwood, VA 24228
540-926-4328

John Flannagan Dam
Route 1, Box 268
Haysi, VA 24256
540-835-9544
(Call for whitewater rafting schedule.)

Drive 20: Abingdon–Big Stone Gap Loop

Abingdon Convention and Visitors'
    Bureau
335 Cummings Street
Abingdon, VA 24210
800-435-3440

Henry W. Meador, Jr. Coal Museum
E. Third Street and Shawnee Avenue
Big Stone Gap, VA 24219
540-523-4950

Jefferson National Forest
Clinch Ranger District
9416 Darden Drive
Wise, VA 24293
540-328-2931

Southwest Virginia Museum
W. First Street and Wood Avenue
Big Stone Gap, VA 24219
540-523-1322

Wise County Chamber of Commerce
765 Park Avenue
Norton, VA 24273
540-679-0961

Drive 21: Mount Rogers Loop

Grayson Highlands State Park
Route 2, Box 141
Mouth of Wilson, VA 24363
540-579-7092

Mount Rogers National Recreation Area
Jefferson National Forest
Route 1, Box 303
Marion, VA 24354
540-783-5196

Drive 22: Cumberland Gap

Cumberland Gap National Historical Park
Box 1848
Middlesboro, KY 40965
606-248-2817

Karlan State Park
Ewing, VA
540-445-3065

Natural Tunnel State Park
Route 1, Box 350
Duffield, VA 24244
540-940-2674

Index

S

T

U

V

About The Author

Bruce Sloane has been a geologist, park ranger, newspaper editor, author, humor columnist, and technical writer. His main writing interests include travel, the natural world, and history. He holds bachelor's and master's degrees in geology. He lives in Rappahannock County, Virginia, not very far from a scenic drive, with his wife, daughter, mother-in-law, dog, and four cats. This is his third book.

FALCONGUIDES® Leading the Way™

FALCONGUIDES® are available for where-to-go hiking, mountain biking, rock climbing, walking, scenic driving, fishing, rockhounding, paddling, birding, wildlife viewing, and camping. We also have FalconGuides on essential outdoor skills and subjects and field identification. The following titles are currently available, but this list grows every year. For a free catalog with a complete list of titles, call FALCON toll-free at 1-800-582-2665.

SCENIC DRIVING GUIDES

Scenic Driving Alaska and the Yukon
Scenic Driving Arizona
Scenic Driving the Beartooth Highway
Scenic Driving California
Scenic Driving Colorado
Scenic Driving Florida
Scenic Driving Georgia
Scenic Driving Hawaii
Scenic Driving Idaho
Scenic Driving Michigan
Scenic Driving Minnesota
Scenic Driving Montana
Scenic Driving New England
Scenic Driving New Mexico
Scenic Driving North Carolina
Scenic Driving Oregon
Scenic Driving the Ozarks
Scenic Driving Pennsylvania
Scenic Driving Texas
Scenic Driving Utah
Scenic Driving Washington
Scenic Driving Wisconsin
Scenic Driving Wyoming
Scenic Driving Yellowstone and
   the Grand Teton National Parks
Scenic Byways East
Scenic Byways Far West
Scenic Byways Rocky Mountains
Back Country Byways

HISTORIC TRAIL GUIDES
Traveling California's Gold Rush Country
Traveling the Lewis & Clark Trail
Traveling the Oregon Trail
Traveler's Guide to the Pony Express Trail

WILDLIFE VIEWING GUIDES
Alaska Wildlife Viewing Guide
Arizona Wildlife Viewing Guide
California Wildlife Viewing Guide
Colorado Wildlife Viewing Guide
Florida Wildlife Viewing Guide
Indiana Wildlife Vewing Guide
Iowa Wildlife Viewing Guide
Kentucky Wildlife Viewing Guide
Massachusetts Wildlife Viewing Guide
Montana Wildlife Viewing Guide
Nebraska Wildlife Viewing Guide
Nevada Wildlife Viewing Guide
New Hampshire Wildlife Viewing Guide
New Jersey Wildlife Viewing Guide
New Mexico Wildlife Viewing Guide
New York Wildlife Viewing Guide
North Carolina Wildlife Viewing Guide
North Dakota Wildlife Viewing Guide
Ohio Wildlife Viewing Guide
Oregon Wildlife Viewing Guide
Puerto Rico & the Virgin Islands
   Wildlife Viewing Guide
Tennessee Wildlife Viewing Guide
Texas Wildlife Viewing Guide
Utah Wildlife Viewing Guide
Vermont Wildlife Viewing Guide
Virginia Wildlife Viewing Guide
Washington Wildlife Viewing Guide
West Virginia Wildlife Viewing Guide
Wisconsin Wildlife Viewing Guide

■ *To order any of these books, check with your local bookseller*
or call FALCON® at 1-800-582-2665.
Visit us on the world wide web at:
www.FalconOutdoors.com

FALCON®

FALCON GUIDES ® Leading the Way™

■ *To order any of these books, check with your local bookseller*
*or call FALCON ® at **1-800-582-2665**.*
Visit us on the world wide web at:
www.FalconOutdoors.com

FALCON®

FALCONGUIDES® Leading the Way

FIELD GUIDES
Bitterroot: Montana State Flower
Canyon Country Wildflowers
Central Rocky Mountains
   Wildflowers
Great Lakes Berry Book
New England Berry Book
Ozark Wildflowers
Pacific Northwest Berry Book
Plants of Arizona
Rare Plants of Colorado
Rocky Mountain Berry Book
Scats & Tracks of the Pacific
   Coast States
Scats & Tracks of the
   Rocky Mountains
Southern Rocky Mountain
   Wildflowers
Tallgrass Prairie Wildflowers
Western Trees
Wildflowers of Southwestern
   Utah
Willow Bark and Rosehips

FISHING GUIDES
Fishing Alaska
Fishing the Beartooths
Fishing Florida
Fishing Glacier National Park
Fishing Maine
Fishing Montana
Fishing Wyoming
Fishing Yellowstone
   National Park

ROCKHOUNDING GUIDES
Rockhounding Arizona
Rockhounding California
Rockhounding Colorado
Rockhounding Montana
Rockhounding Nevada
Rockhound's Guide to New
   Mexico
Rockhounding Texas
Rockhounding Utah
Rockhounding Wyoming

MORE GUIDEBOOKS
Backcountry Horseman's
   Guide to Washington
Camping California's
   National Forests
Exploring Canyonlands &
   Arches National Parks
Exploring Hawaii's Parklands
Exploring Mount Helena
Exploring Southern California
   Beaches
Recreation Guide to WA
   National Forests
Touring California & Nevada
   Hot Springs
Touring Colorado Hot Springs
Touring Montana & Wyoming
   Hot Springs
Trail Riding Western
   Montana
Wild Country Companion
Wilderness Directory
Wild Montana
Wild Utah

BIRDING GUIDES
Birding Minnesota
Birding Montana
Birding Northern California
Birding Texas
Birding Utah

PADDLING GUIDES
Floater's Guide to Colorado
Paddling Minnesota
Paddling Montana
Paddling Okefenokee
Paddling Oregon
Paddling Yellowstone & Grand
   Teton National Parks

HOW-TO GUIDES
Avalanche Aware
Backpacking Tips
Bear Aware
Desert Hiking Tips
Hiking with Dogs
Leave No Trace
Mountain Lion Alert
Reading Weather
Route Finding
Using GPS
Wilderness First Aid
Wilderness Survival

WALKING
Walking Colorado Springs
Walking Denver
Walking Portland
Walking St. Louis
Walking Virginia Beach

■ *To order any of these books, check with your local bookseller*
*or call FALCON ® at **1-800-582-2665**.*
Visit us on the world wide web at:
www.FalconOutdoors.com

FALCON®

It Happened in *Series from TwoDot Books*

An imprint of Falcon Publishing

TWODOT

Featured in this series are fascinating stories about events that helped shape each state's history. Written in a lively, easy-to-read style, each book features 31-34 stories for history buffs of all ages. Entertaining and informative, each book is 6x9", features b&w illustrations, and is only $8.95.

It Happened in Arizona
It Happened in Colorado
It Happened in Montana
It Happened in New Mexico
It Happened in Oregon
It Happened in Southern California
It Happened in Texas
It Happened in Utah
It Happened in Washington

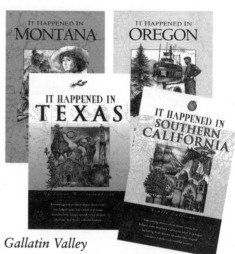

More from TwoDot Books

Bozeman and the Gallatin Valley
Charlie's Trail: The Life and Art of C.M. Russell
Flight of the Dove: The Story of Jeannette Rankin
Growing up Western
Heart of the Trail: The Stories of Eight Wagon Train Women
Jeannette Rankin: Bright Star in the Big Sky
Men with Sand: Great Explorers of the American West
Montana Campfire Tales: Fourteen Historical Essays
More Than Petticoats: Remarkable Montana Women
More Than Petticoats: Rmarkable Oregon Women
More Than Petticoats: Remarkable Washington Women
The Champion Buffalo Hunter
The Only Good Bear is a Dead Bear
Today I Baled Some Hay to Feed the Sheep the Coyotes Eat

The TwoDot line features classic western literature and history. Each book celebrates and interprets the vast spaces and rich culture of the American West.

FALCON®

To order check with your local bookseller or call Falcon at

1-800-582-2665

Ask for a FREE catalog featuring a complete list of titles on nature, outdoor recreation, travel and the West.